West Pointer to Imprisoned Preacher... WHY?

Penuel Kodesh

ISBN 978-1-64191-915-9 (paperback)
ISBN 978-1-64191-916-6 (digital)

Copyright © 2018 by Penuel Kodesh

All rights reserved. No part of this publication may be reproduced, distributed, or transmitted in any form or by any means, including photocopying, recording, or other electronic or mechanical methods without the prior written permission of the publisher. For permission requests, solicit the publisher via the address below.

Christian Faith Publishing, Inc.
832 Park Avenue
Meadville, PA 16335
www.christianfaithpublishing.com

Printed in the United States of America

"…a powerful message…God is behind the scene…"

Pastor Herb Robertson
A parolee (35 years in prison)

"Impressive!"

Chaplain (Ret.) Don Stine
Buckingham Prison, Virginia

"A great book…written by the inspiration of our God. Every Christian and military personnel, especially those who have been through numerous traumatic experiences while serving the Country, should read it."

Jin Lee, Major (Ret.), US Army,
A Fellow Artilleryman

"A moving story of tragedy, sorrow, and redemption. After reading this book, no one should doubt the power of Christ and His Paschal Mystery to bring light into even the darkest places of our hearts."

Christus Vincit,
Fr. Louis H. Thomas
St. Charles Parish, Ohio

"A story of turn-around…Ken is truly making a positive impact as a result of horrific, life-changing event."

Mark Coats, Ken's 1st West Point Roommate
Colonel (Ret.), US Army
Combat Engineer, 1st Armored Division
Engineer Planner, V Corps
Desert Shield/Storm, Operations Iraqi Freedom

"A powerful, troubling, disquieting chronicle about redemption and both divine and human forgiveness…very interesting and illuminating with regards to one military veteran's trials and tribulations."

Kirk E. Murray, Lt. Colonel (Ret.), US Army
VP Global OutReach, FamilyLife

"This extraordinary book should illuminate the hearts of those walking through the dark valley of despair and remind us of Apostle Paul whose life was transformed through God's indescribable redemptive and restorative power…a very interesting, challenging and triumphant story of overcoming unthinkable adversities and tribulations"

Chan Hyo Park, Ph.D. & R.Ph.
Retired (32 years), US Federal Government

"A must read…it should be enlightening, especially those legally challenged."

Christian Brother "Mo"
US Navy Veteran in the Veterans POD
Buckingham Correctional Center, Virginia

"May [the writings of my mind], the words of my mouth and the meditation of my heart be pleasing in your sight, O LORD, my Rock and my Redeemer." (Psalms 19:14)

Caveat

Honest attempts have been made to accurately and timely capture all thoughts of the subject prisoner, Kenston (Ken, the Joe) Kangson Yi, into this book. Overcoming all unavoidable limitations in the prison environment has been very challenging but hopefully rewarding for all in the near future.

Translation Copyright

Under copyright regulations, this book may not be translated and/or printed without a written permission from the JoeAnna Ministries (JAM) and the Joyful Mission Network (JMN). 100% of the royalty from this book will be used to support the mission of the JAM/JMN, and your understanding and compliance of the copyright regulations will be appreciated.

An extraordinary story of redemption and hope, a second chance.

"The prisoner who had lost faith in the future—his future—was doomed."
(Dr. Viktor Frankl, a Holocaust survivor)

Dedication

The subject's deceased wife, YI "Hannah" Hyon-chong, and deceased adopted daughter, YI Joy Ja-hyon.

All who are invisibly and quietly suffering from mental illnesses and their supportive family members and friends.

Contents

Acknowledgments 15

Foreword 17

Prologue 31

Chapter 1:   Malicious Motives? 41

Chapter 2:   Resume, Job Application 44

Chapter 3:   Repentance 50

Chapter 4:   Forgiveness, Asking for Mercy! 56

Chapter 5:   My Story Is Your Story! 61

Chapter 6:   Hope: A Second Chance! 66

Chapter 7:   Why Jesus? 69

Chapter 8:   Oh, Jesus Was Never in Hell! 90

Chapter 9:   Oh, The Sabbath Is Not Saturday! 101

Chapter 10: Oh, Tithing Should Be Voluntary! 116

Chapter 11: How Could They Do That? 123

Conclusions 139

Epilogue 143

A Brief Remark for the Graduation Ceremony
     (Nov. 18, 2016) 149

A Synopsis of the Story 151

The Purpose of the Book = I^3 153

What's Hot Next? 155

Acknowledgments

This book acknowledges everyone who has remembered "Ken, the Dreaming Joseph (Joe)," the subject in the book, and supported him. The publication of the book could not be possible without their support. The list is very long; thus, only top seven groups are mentioned below:

1) YI Ki-son "Jacob" and CHUNG Su-tok Susan "Rachel," the most loving parents;
2) YI Charlie Kang-hui, the youngest brother, and his family, who have endured so much to this day;
3) PARK "Anna" Hi-sook, the first partner minister of the JoeAnna Ministries (JoeAnna.org) and other faithful ministry partners like her;
4) The Veterans POD Church and the Buckingham Christian Fellowship (Dillwyn, Virginia);
5) Kirk Murray, a dear friend from Immanuel Bible Church (Springfield, Virginia), and so many other good friends like him;
6) Fr. Louis H. Thomas and Stanley S. Thomas, the beloved twin brothers adopted from Korea and raised by a loving single parent, Mommy Sun-hui;
7) MOON Myung-ja and many prayer warriors. She is named here as a comforting and fervent role model residing in Cleveland, Ohio.

Foreword

You will not be disappointed in reading this book. It should exhume and arouse life-transforming humanity, compassion, and empathy in you. You should consider that "Penuel Kodesh," the author of this book, and "Ken, the Joe," are speaking in one voice. We look for no excuses, no commiseration, no sympathy, or no pity. We pray for you to experience heartbreaking and treasured moments because the story in this book could be yours.

Here, two testimonials from Mongolia are shared. Ever since Ken has been incarcerated, the land and the people of Mongolia have been in his mind to reach out. The bottom line is that he has financially and prayerfully supported two ministries in Mongolia. Testimonies from a native Mongolian, Pastor Puje Khaltar, and a Korean-American missionary couple, Jay and Roxanne Lee, should interest you in that even a prisoner in a constrained environment with so many limitations can touch many lives in a country six thousand miles away.

As you will learn in this book, Ken has formed a strategic partnership with Pastor Puje, who pastors two churches in Ulaanbaatar, Mongolia (JoeAnna.org/Mongolia). Even in prison with "the chessboard and a notebook,"[1] Ken is able to communicate frequently with his Mongolian partner and multiple ministry partners to fulfill his strategic vision, "Global Evangelism through the Joyful Mission Network," which is etched on the backside of the chessboard.

---

[1] Ken often refers the backside of the chessboard and a pocket calendar book as his prison office.

PENUEL KODESH

Here is Pastor Puje's testimony as a start.

> *My name is Pastor Paul Puje in Ulaanbaatar, Mongolia. I am a pastor of New Future Church, ministering to the needy children, and the Light of Life Church, ministering to the homeless.*
>
> *By the grace of God and His provisions, I was able to care for my own family of six and the church family of over 230. I have experienced many divine miracles during my twenty-four years of ministries, but I just like to share one miracle God has given me through the JoeAnna Ministries (JAM). I hope and pray that you get blessed with my sharing.*
>
> *First, when my first son was suffering from serious epilepsy in need of high funds to pay for the expensive medicine, Minister Kenston Yi of JAM reached out to us. Through his generous giving of 4,000 USD my son was completely healed from epilepsy. My son's treatment was very expensive; without anyone's help, we could not survive. Every month, we spent more than a thousand dollars for our son's treatment for five years, but our income was not high. Our living expenses were high. We sold out almost all our things for Joshua's treatment. In that time, Ken transferred money to our account. In that time, we did not know each other, but he sent money to us. We believe God sent him to us.*
>
> *Second, during the recent Christmas holidays, we were behind in paying our apartment rent and the landlord had cut off the electricity. The weather was freezing cold, and my family had suffered a suspenseful moment. But the JAM once again came to deliver us. The rent was paid, and my family was*

safe and comfortable. I asked our landlord to wait to cut off our electricity because I have a ministry partner who will send us money.

Third, Minister Ken had been reaching out to me on a daily basis, encouraging me and giving me hope for the future. We have a common vision to minister not only unto my people in Mongolia, but also all other neighboring nations. Almost every night, I talked to Ken on the phone. I was praying God for a mentor, but God already sent me Ken. I was ministering for many years. I was burned out, but after I started to talk to him on the phone, I became normal and was encouraged, and I wanted to do more ministry. He suggested to me to do work balance and spend time with family members. I decided to follow his suggestions.

Love in Christ,
Puje

The second testimony is from Missionary Jay and Roxanne. Their amazing missionary journey is available at JRoxLee.WordPress.com, and here is just a snapshot of remarkable works happening in their family and ministries.

Hi! This is Roxanne. That bleak January day when I found out I had a fist-sized fibroid on the outside of my uterus, I wasn't really worried. I decided to stop by a store to pick up some groceries. There, I met a Korean friend who works at Mongolian International University (MIU). I told her the news, and she went straight home and started calling people. Within a week, she arranged for me to meet some medical missionaries who scanned all my major organs via ultrasound for free. They said no doctor in Mongolia had the tools to do laparoscopic surgery, so I had better go to Korea. Within a month, Jay and this loving group of MIU staff had set everything up. We decided Jay should come to Korea with me for translation and advocacy. So I wrote an extensive list of chores and meal plans for the kids and prayed the Lord would keep them safe for the five days that Jay would be with me.

We met Dr. Bomjay Choi the first day. He was a joyful and energetic man who reassured us that he would take good care of me. The next day, a CT scan showed the mass to be much larger than the ultrasound measurements, and I was worried that they'd have to cut open my abdomen to remove it, which was the big reason I was not having the surgery done in Mongolia. I told him I was scared, and he said, "Don't be scared. Trust me and trust the Lord." And he motioned to a crucifix on the wall of his office.

WEST POINTER TO IMPRISONED PREACHER... WHY?

The surgery went well, and the pain and nausea soon passed. Jay had to leave the day after the surgery to go back and teach at MIU and take care of the kids. I stayed longer to travel back to Mongolia with the team from Creation and Love Women's Hospital (CLWH) that was going there.

CLWH has opened a branch in Mongolia, and they are going to open one in Nepal. They may have others that I do not know of because they have translators on staff to help Chinese, Russian, Uzbek, and Mongolians seeking his expertise in fertility.

CLWH gave us a discount because we are m-workers so that the total bill for my surgery and hospital stay of fifteen days was $3,000. If we add in the $1,000 for plane tickets and other travel expenses, that is only $4,000. God is so amazing. Someone gave a gift in December for the surgery, and they (and we) didn't even know I had a tumor. Then our sending church sent enough to cover our travel expenses.

I hope you can see by reading this that the Lord is lavish in his love, present with his people, and masterful in his planning. You can trust him for he will never fail. All glory be to Jesus!

Hi! This is Jay. In September, my vision of "A Dorm for Discipleship" came true when we opened our first dormitory. Five young women now live in a four-bedroom, one-bathroom apartment about two miles from Mongolia International University. We believe God has led us to help these students by giving them a gift greater than housing; we are teaching them how to study God's word, how to live in community, and how to worship Jesus Christ. Roxanne teaches the Bible once a week, and our whole family holds house church with the students once a week. Our hope is that we can open another dormitory for young men by the beginning of next academic year.

We've named the first Discipleship Dorm as Dormitory 104 because that is the door number of the apartment we are using. Creative, right? Below are two students' biographies.

"I am twenty-one years old. I grew up in a town three hours from the capital city of Mongolia. I moved to Ulaanbaatar in 2013 to enroll at Mongolia International University. I am a junior majoring in International Management. I met Jay Bagsh at MIU, and he told me about the dorm idea. I felt good when I heard about it because of the location and price. I moved into Dormitory 104 in October 2016. The best thing about living in there is the location and learning a lot of things. I have learned how to read and understand the Bible from Roxanne's Bible studies. From the house church, I have known more about Jesus and history." (Sophia*)

"I am eighteen years old. I grew up in Ulaanbaatar. I am a freshman majoring in International Management. I felt very excited when I heard about the dorm idea because my place exists near the international airport, which is quite far from MIU, so I need around two hours to get to school. I moved into Dormitory 104 in October. The best thing about living there is learning the Bible, also getting the information about Jesus, having a good relationship with my mates, realizing how to live by myself. I have learned verses of John and Hebrews from Roxanne's Bible studies. From the

WEST POINTER TO IMPRISONED PREACHER… WHY?

house church, I have learned who is the Son of God, how he was greater than other ones, he could do anything, also quite a lot of verses of Bible especially verses of Hebrews, John, and Matthew." (Michelle*)
  *Names have been changed to protect identity. Please pray for this outreach to bear much fruit as students learn what it means to become a disciple of Jesus Christ. Each pays around $30 per month; the amount is a token of each tenant's commitment and appreciation, but it by no means covers the expenses. If you'd like to sponsor any of the tenants individually, just mention Dormitory 104 when you call Pioneers: 1.800.755.7284. Thank you!

Now that you are familiar with how Ken has impacted the needy serving hands in Mongolia, we should move on to his story. Before the story begins, the author strongly feels that the reader should be informed of startling statistics of military veterans committing suicide each day because Ken's story is about his failed multiple suicide attempts and a familicide attempt. In addition, for your situational awareness, we want to share another astounding statistic of deteriorating mental health of the kids in America. As an informed reader, you should be able to flip through the pages with clear understanding of the purpose in writing this book. So let us begin the literary expedition.

USA Today reported in 2016, "A 2010 calculation by the VA[2] estimates that 22 veterans kill themselves each day. The VA, which has not updated that estimate, says the hotline rescues 30 veterans from suicide each day."[3]

---

[2] VA is an acronym for the US Department of Veterans Affairs, which has been a controversial administration of the President of the United States of America aka POTUS.

[3] From an article titled, "Email Shows VA Hotline Failed Vets" in *USA Today*, July 1, 2016.

Furthermore, *Disabled American Veterans (DAV) Magazine* has recently reported, "An examination of more than 55 million nationwide records from 1979 to 2014 provided the Department of Veterans Affairs with the most extensive data to date on veteran suicide in the United States. The report states an average of 20 veterans dies by suicide each day. Only six are users of VA services."[4] The article quotes a lamentation from Dr. Caitlin Thompson, Executive Director, VA Office of Suicide Prevention, "When 20 veterans die by suicide and 14 veterans hadn't touched VA care, it means that we can't do this alone."[5]

Now we feel that you are attentive to the disturbing reality of uncontainable suicides committed by military veterans, you should also keep in mind that Ken could have been a part of such an alarming suicide statistic because he is a veteran himself. As you will note in Ken's military career in Chapter 2, "Resume, Job Application," his thirty-year military history in the US Army began in 1979 and ended in 2009.

As you will learn in this book, Ken had attempted to commit suicide multiple times. His triumphal story involves such deadly mental illness which requires timely, reliable, and professional mental health treatment. When such illness is not treated properly, it could turn fatal to the suffering, sufferer's family and friends, or the society as a whole. Ken's family had suffered such mental disease, and the result was a fatal family tragedy. As you continue in the story, you will become more aware of the seriousness of such a poisonous mental disease.

In addition to exposing you to the startling statistics of the military suicides, we want you to be aware of deteriorating mental health condition in our kids in America. They are the future of this country, and we should do something about it. We want to share an article from the *Time* magazine under the title, "The Kids Are Not All Right."

---

[4] Charity Edgar, 20 TOO MANY, How new figures are steering VA suicide prevention efforts, *DAV MAGAZINE* January/February 2017, P.12.
[5] Ibid. p.12.

WEST POINTER TO IMPRISONED PREACHER... WHY?

In the Mental Health section of the magazine, Susanna Schrasdorff reports, "In 2015, about 3 million teens ages 12 to 17 had had at least one major depressive episodes in the past year, according to the Department of Health and Human Services. More than 2 million report experiencing depression that impairs their daily function. About 30% of girls and 20% of boys–totaling 6.3 million teens–have had an anxiety disorder, according to data from the National Institute of Mental Health."[6]

Why share the deteriorating mental health of American kids? Ken could have struggled with similar mental health issues during his youth as he had coped with a major culture shock, resulting from a traumatic immigration to America from Korea at the age of fifteen. According to his words, washing dishes at a Chinese restaurant at the age of sixteen was therapeutic. It was a major coping mechanism about which he has never told anyone.

Ken knew that all things were stacked against him as he had struggled in the new world with the language barrier and the culture shock. He needed the higher power, and he found such power in Christianity. He imagined and believed that this Christian God, the Almighty El-Shaddai, could help him overcome the barrier, the shock, the insecurity, the hopelessness, and so forth. Ken thought that the Korean-American community and his parents with seriously broken English and low income were not the sources where the help could come for him to succeed.

They all were depressing, and Ken had to get out the area real fast. Then he finally found the escape. His enlisting in the US Army and reporting to a boot camp at Fort Knox, Kentucky, just three days after his high school graduation, was the way out of the depressive environment. It was clearly an ultimate coping attempt, the only way to get out of the gloomy community.

Now the book may even begin to sound depressive; however, the purpose of this book is to inform, illuminate, and inspire you. We want you to be aware of deadly mental illnesses and their conse-

---

[6] Susanna Schrasdorff. "The Kids Are Not All Right," *Time* (November 7, 2016) p.47

quences when left untreated properly and timely. Although this book is not intended to proselytize you to become a Christian, the second purpose of this book is to shed some insight into the mystery of the so-called Gospel in the Bible. It is very important to mention here that Ken strongly testifies that the true healing comes from serving others. He is talking about the healing from not only the mental illnesses, but also all other illnesses. So we should all ask ourselves, "What have we done lately to serve fellow human beings?"

Finally, the intention of this book will be served when you are inspired by the heartrending story of one ordinary man's audacious journey as a naive immigrant boy from war-torn Korea, a daring cadet at the prestigious United States Military Academy at West Point, a thirty-year veteran of an illustrative military career, a survivor of the 9/11 terror attack, a sufferer of such compounding and aggravating mental illness brought on by the attack, a victim of the broken VA medical care system, incarcerated from a fatal family tragedy, an inescapable familicide, stalked by the failed system (in the mind of the author), a called minister of the Christian gospel while imprisoned, and a visionary to fulfill a God-given global outreach serving the hurt, both visible and invisible through the Joyful Mission Network.[7]

In order to help you navigate through the book, you should familiarize with key contextual vocabularies which are not normally understood by the society. This author feels that the terms such as murder, insanity, panic attack, clinical depression, etc., need to be defined. Moreover, to help you start you off optimistically, the following quotes are prayerfully shared to give you awareness and hope:

---

[7] Ken Yi has written down his vision according to Habakkuk 2:2 on JoeAnna.org and other media. His vision is "Global Evangelism thru the Joyful Mission Network" where Joyful honors his deceased daughter Joy Yi.

WEST POINTER TO IMPRISONED PREACHER... WHY?

Hello, Mr. Ken (Joe) Yi,

I was encouraged by your letter where I find you witnessing in the lion's den. Keep up the great work that you are doing. Congratulation on getting closer to obtaining your degree. Never let your current location determine how high you can fly.

Mr. Terry Wiggins
First Sergeant (Ret.), US Army
Veterans Advocate, the Department of Corrections
The Commonwealth of Virginia

Dear Kenston,

You've helped us tremendously and advanced the work of the Lord in ways we will not know until we get to heaven.

Jay and Roxanne Lee
Missionaries in Mongolia through Pioneers.Com

Now to set the stage for your smooth and informative reading, the following words from Ken's mother-in-law (a victim's mother) and Ken's counsel are shared. Ken is not looking for any excuses as you will find in his testimonial letters as you turn the pages, he is simply looking for your empathy, the benefit of doubt, and a second chance, which is the grace and mercy from not only above, but also your heart.

> *"When my 'Sa-Bu-In' [Ken's mother] called me to inform the death of my daughter without mentioning the killer was my 'Sa-wee' [Ken] himself, I immediately uttered my Sa-wee's mental illness led to the death of my daughter."*
>
> KIM Sun-ae,[8] mother-in-law of Ken, the Joe

---

[8] Notarized petition for Ken's clemency dated May 26, 2014, was addressed to the Governor of Virginia as so enclosed in Chapter 4, "Forgiveness, Asking for Mercy!"

WEST POINTER TO IMPRISONED PREACHER... WHY?

When the Virginia Court of Appeals ruled contrary to settled precedent by holding that the excited utterance of the victim's mother was not admissible at trial, the following reason was filed in Petition for Rehearing after Refusal of Petition for Appeal[9]:

> *"This Court's decision in Pugh v. Commonwealth, 223 Va. 663 (1982), established that being informed of the death of one's child is a 'startling event' such that the statement that follows is an excited utterance. The Court of Appeal affirmed the trial court's ruling excluding from testimony the victim's mother's outburst blaming Yi's mental illness for the death of her daughter before anyone had even told her that it was a homicide. This statement was powerful evidence of the extent to which Yi's severe mental illness was known to his family. It refuted any claim of fabrication or exaggeration on the part of the defendant. Yet it went unheard by the jury, and Yi was consequently denied a trial worthy of confidence."*
>
>
>
> *Patrick M. Blanch, Esq.*
> *Counsel for Kenston Yi*
>
>

---

[9] Petition for Rehearing after Refusal of Petition for Appeal was filed in the Supreme Court of Virginia and a copy furnished to the Office of the Attorney General of the Commonwealth of Virginia on October 18, 2013.

The mental illness when left untreated can destroy families. Such tragedy had struck the family of a state senator:

> *"The stabbing of Virginia State Sen. Creigh Deeds apparently by his son, Gus, who later committed suicide, is the latest in a string of mental health related violence. Deeds, 24, didn't get the help he needed."*
>
> *Mr. Pete Earley at www.peterearley.com*
> *Author of CRAZY: A Father's Service Through America's Mental Health Madness*

Sen. Deeds' empathy toward Ken's tragedy and the senator's willingness to do to something about the broken mental health system are shown in the following statement:

Dear Mr. and Mrs. Yi,

I am so very sorry about your own personal loss and was heartbroken to read the story of your son, daughter-in-law, and granddaughter. I am humbled and honored by your support for my efforts to improve the mental health system here in Virginia, and hopefully nationwide.

Honorable Creigh Deeds[10] *Virginia State Senator*

---

[10] Senator Deed's son, Gus Deeds, committed suicide on November 13, 2013, after stabbing his dad more than ten times in the head and neck.

Prologue

Kenston (Ken) Kangson Yi, aka the Dreaming Joseph (Joe), the subject in this book, is serving a forty-year sentence for the first-degree double murder conviction.[11] "First degree" means the murder was premeditated. Ken refused the guilty plea offer of the second degree manslaughter with maximum of 20-year sentencing. To this day, he declares "Not Guilty by the Reason of Insanity (NGRI)." The reader is highly recommended to reserve any personal condemnation or judgment of the subject until this book is thoroughly read and meditate upon the following words:

"This is the verdict: Light has come into the world, but men loved darkness instead of light because their deeds were evil." (John 3:19)

Jesus, who claimed to be the Messiah. (John 4:25–26)

"There is now no condemnation for those who are in Christ Jesus because through Christ Jesus the law of Spirit of life set me free from the law of sin and death." (Romans 8:1–2)

Apostle Paul, a converted murderer. (Acts 22:4)

---

[11] Twenty years for each first-degree murder is the minimum sentence. The maximum is life without parole. Some with one first-degree murder conviction serve multiple life sentences. Some serve forty years for an offense that does not involve murder. These facts show that the jury was somewhat empathetic toward Ken, and the judge took the recommended twenty-year sentence by the jury. So the forty-year sentence was imposed on Ken.

Keeping in mind that this book is neither jurisprudential nor medical in nature, we feel warranted to share the definition of "Insanity, Survivor Guilt, Panic Attack, Insomnia, and Clinical Depression" to help the reader better understand the scope of this book whose underlying basis are these highly misunderstood diagnoses of mental illnesses that Ken, the Joe, had deeply suffered.

Insanity[12]

1) Webster's Third New International Dictionary: "the state of being insane: unsoundness or derangement of the mind... such unsoundness of mind or lack of understanding as prevents one from having the mental capacity required by law to enter into a particular relationship, status, or transaction, or as excuses one from criminal or civil responsibility."
2) Black's Law Dictionary: "a social and legal term rather than a medical one, and indicates a condition which renders the affected person unfit to enjoy liberty of action because of the unreliability of his behavior with concomitant danger to himself and others...more or less synonymous with mental illness or psychosis. In law, the tem is used to denote that degree of mental illness which negates the individual's legal responsibility or capacity."

The reader should keep in mind that Ken has already repented of the evil acts of taking the precious lives of his own family members; however, he has not recanted the plea of Not Guilty by the Reason of Insanity (NGRI). In Ken's mind, although he has asked for forgiveness from his Creator God and the victim's family, his mother-in-law's, and received the forgiveness, he does not owe any apology

---

[12] Ken's plea has been Not Guilty by the Reason of Insanity (NGRI); thus, the reader should understand what the meaning of "Insanity" is.

legally. Ken's case was a mental issue, a medical one; nonetheless, the case had lost the mental health focus and decided on the legal focus.

Legally, Ken was determined to be sane at the time of the tragic moments. However, by the aforementioned definition of insanity, Ken continues to plead innocent. He says, "No sane person could make such heinous familicide attempt, and only sane person with malicious motives can perform such atrocious murders." The court has never proven any motives for the murders, and the only thing Ken gained from such appalling killings were a family tragedy.

Survivor Guilt

The Good Therapy blog site has a wealth of information about Survivor Guilt, which relates to a mental sickness known as Post-Traumatic Stress Disorder (PTSD). This author feels that the reader should understand what Survivor Guilt is as you thumb through this book. You may be experiencing the guilt or you may know someone who is suffering from it. The subject of this book had intensely suffered from the guilt, and his guilt may be subdued at the moment.

"Survivor guilt is a particular type of guilt that may develop in people who have survived a life-threatening situation. Individuals who believe it is unfair that they survived when others died and/or believe they did not do enough to save the lives of others may come to experience survivor guilt after trauma or a catastrophic event

…survivor guilt has been identified in veterans, those who survived the Holocaust, 9/11 survivors, first responders, and transplant recipients…survivor guilt can develop following a small-scale event (such as a car accident in which only some people died or when a loved one dies by suicide) or larger-scale tragedies (such as the 9/11 terrorist attacks or mass shootings). Symptoms of survivor guilt typically include nightmares, difficulty sleeping, flashbacks to the traumatic event. Loss of motivation, irritability, a sense of numbness, and thoughts about the meaning of life … Those who survive may transform their feelings of guilt into a sense of increased meaning and purpose. They may also use survivor guilt as a way to cope with the feelings of helplessness and powerlessness that can occur in traumatic situations."[13]

Ken had experienced the 9/11 terrorist attack at Pentagon where 184 innocent lives were lost and many were injured both physically and mentally. Ken and other injured will probably never recover completely from this "Survivor Guilt" mental illness.

Ken's surviving the 9/11 terrorists attack is just compounding "Survivor Guilt" illness. The author feels it is very fitting to mention Ken's mental struggle in relation to "Survivor Guilt."

Apostle John recorded Jesus' famous maxim that even the non-Christians echo to make a point that actions do speak louder than words: "Greater love has no one than this, that he lay down his life for his friends." (John 15:13) Ultimately, Jesus did lay down his own life for the lost humanity.

Likewise, many lives were laid down in hostile territories to preserve the American values such as liberty and justice for all. When these fallen lives are close to you, their lives would mean so much more to you. Moreover, you may even experience "Survivor Guilt" symptoms.

Similarly, Ken felt such guilt whenever these fallen bodies were brought home in coffins draped in American flags. Especially when his revered old boss (a two-star general), dedicated friends, and dutiful West Point classmates return home in such tragic but heroic manner, Ken's guilt has been demonstrated by helpless heavy tears and big lumps in his throat.

Ken's "Survivor Guilt" had intensified during his tireless support of Operations Enduring Freedom, Operations Iraqi Freedom, Global War on Terrorism and other contingency operations. Then when poorly armored military vehicles that Ken had staffed diligently and stressfully fielded into the conflict zones were being blown up

---

[13] The description of Survivor Guilt retrieved from www.goodtherapy.org/blog/psychpedia/survivor-guilt?simpleview=1

by Improvised Explosive Devices (IEDs) perishing many lives, disintegrating countless limbs and destroying numerous minds (PTSD symptoms), Ken's mind was also helplessly and hopelessly crushed.

Even more severe "Survivor Guilt" arouse when Ken has hopelessly felt inability to live up to the maxim to lay his life sanely for his own family. Insanely laying down his own life, a humiliating and disgraceful suicidal deed, would have had a devastating effect on his family.

Most certainly during his darkest moments, Ken could not let his own family suffer as a result of his ludicrous laying down of his own life. In his insane mind, the familicide was the only option available. Ken's corrupted mind was chasing after him with repeated fatal whispers, "There is no way out!"

Panic Attacks

Mayo Clinic provides informative and preventative descriptions of the attacks and disorder. The description relevant to this book is quoted below:

"Panic attacks and panic disorder begin suddenly, without warning. They can strike at any time—when you're driving a car, at the mall, sound asleep or in the middle of a business meeting. You may have occasional panic attacks or they may occur frequently.

Panic attacks typically include some of these symptoms: sense of impending doom or danger, fear of loss of control or death, rapid, pounding heart rate, trembling or shaking, shortness of breath or tightness in your throat, dizziness, lightheadedness or faintness.

One of the worst things about panic attacks is the intense fear that you'll have another one. If you have panic attack symptoms, seek medical help as soon as possible. Panic attacks, while intensely uncomfortable, are not dangerous. But panic attacks are hard to manage on your own, and they may get worse without treatment."[14]

---

[14] Mayo Clinic Staff, "Diseases and conditions, Panic attacks and panic disorder," Mayo Clinic.

Ken did not know he had been suffering from panic attacks. Whenever his heart was palpitating, he had thought he was having heart attacks. The family medicine and emergency doctors whom Ken had seen could not diagnose Ken's illnesses as mental health issues.

Only trained and certified mental health treatment professionals can understand the symptoms of mental illnesses that Ken and any other mentally ill people can describe. Understanding what panic attacks are, the reader or anyone experiencing such attack should seek proper and timely mental health treatments.

Insomnia

Mayo Clinic Family Health Book warns the consequences of insomnia that about one-third of all people experience during their stressful living.

Instead of sharing the definition of commonly known insomnia, the author wishes to reiterate commonly unknown consequences of the sleep disorder.

"For most people, a night or two of poor sleep, or even a night of no sleep, isn't that bad. Lost sleep may sap your motivation and make it difficult to concentrate, but as long as you get back to a normal sleep schedule within a few days, you'll experience no lasting consequences. One good night of sleep after few poor ones usually is enough to catch up.

However, chronically losing sleep can result in sleep debt, which can lead to serious consequences. Sleep debt is cumulative, and even small nightly sleep losses can add up to affect daytime function. Possible consequences include increased accidents and poor performance on the job or in school.

Long-term sleep deprivation can affect your physical and mental health. Sleep helps bolster your immune system so that you can fight off viruses and bacteria. After a few nights of absolutely no sleep, some people begin hallucinating."[15]

Here, it is important to note that Ken had suffered from serious insomnia for 120 days using his own uttered words, "Four months!" to the mental and medical health treatment professionals. One occasion at the Fort Belvoir emergency room, Ken was begging the ER doctor on duty, "Please put me to sleep for just two hours!"

On another occasion, during a sick call as a retiree at the DeWitt Army Hospital, he was begging to see the mental health professional. The doctor on duty called a psychologist on duty who replied, "I cannot see him because he is a retiree." Since Ken was no longer on active duty status, his desperate mental health issue could not be attended at the hospital. Such incident was a mental blow to Ken, who had already attempted to see the Veterans Affairs providers who are not easily accessible.

Then the doctor prescribed twenty days' worth of controlled Ambien pills to help Ken sleep. After literally signing for the pills at the pharmacy window, he had struggled to sleep for few nights without success. Ultimately, the remaining thirteen to fourteen pills were swallowed in an attempt to commit a suicide on that darkest day. Ken just wanted to sleep and never wake up!

Clinical Depression

Clinical depression is different from general depression. Clinical depression requires the treatments of mental health professionals. Unless treated timely and properly, the fatal results could occur from such dangerous illnesses. People suffering from clinical depression may have both suicidal and homicidal thoughts under which Ken was suffering. His mental suffering was untreated in a timely manner and a proper fashion.

---

[15] Scott C. Litin, MD, "Mayo Clinic Family Health Book," (New York: 2005), p.1253.

Mayo Clinic also provides excellent information about major depressive disorder relevant to this book. The following quotation comes from Mayo Clinic Staff:

"Although depression may occur only one time during your life, usually people have multiple episodes of depression. During these episodes, symptoms occur most of the day, nearly every day and may include feeling of sadness, tearfulness, emptiness, hopelessness, angry outbursts, irritability, frustration, even over small matters, loss of interest or pleasure in most or all normal activities, such as sex, hobbies or sports, sleep disturbances, including insomnia…anxiety, agitation or restlessness, slow thinking, speaking or body movements, feelings of worthlessness or guilt, fixating on past failures or blaming yourself for things that aren't your responsibility…frequent or recurrent thoughts of death, suicidal thoughts, suicide attempts or suicide, unexplained physical problems, such as back pain or headaches…

If you feel depressed, make an appointment to see your doctor as soon as you can. If you're reluctant to seek treatment, talk to a friend or loved one, a health care professional, a faith leader, or someone else you trust.

If you think you may hurt yourself or attempt suicide, call 911 or your local emergency number immediately. Also consider these options if you're having suicidal thoughts: call your mental health specialist…a suicide hotline number…1-800-273-TALK (1-800-273-8255). Use that same number and press 1 to reach the Veterans Crisis Line."[16]

Now after sharing with the reader what Insanity, Survivor Guilt, Panic Attack, Insomnia, and Clinical Depression mean, this author feels confident that you as the reader have general awareness of the mental disorder terminologies relevant to the book. Here we want to close the prologue and begin exploring Ken's story where you can gleam from his writings since his incarceration on June 14, 2010.

---

[16] Ibid.

WEST POINTER TO IMPRISONED PREACHER... WHY?

The reader should be aware that this book is not a list of cheap excuses for the atrocious killings that Ken, the Joe, had committed. He is extremely remorseful about the horrific acts. Regardless, he had already asked for forgiveness from his Creator and the victim's family (Ken's mother-in-law's) who had graciously reconciled with Ken. The family had already petitioned in 2014 to the Governor of Virginia[17] for pardoning Ken; however, the petition packet has been on hold per Ken's desire to tell the true story first. Thus, the story now begins.

---

[17] The entire petition packet should be available at the time of this book's publication at JoeAnna.org/Petition.

CHAPTER 1

Malicious Motives?

Why the killings? What were the motives? If so, were they malicious? What was gained by the killings? Obviously, nobody can dispute the fact that we, human beings, are motivated by something to act in certain ways. The best way to explain the absent and unproven malicious motives in Ken's case is to compare the malicious motives demonstrated by biblical murderers such as Prophet Moses, King David, and Apostle Paul, who wrote the most revered books in the Bible.

Although apparent malicious motives in taking innocent people's lives were written in their stories in the Bible, God used them to write the significant portion of the Bible. They all answered the calling from their Creator. Then the lives of Moses, David, and Paul were forever changed, and their stories have continued to transform the lives of so many. Ken was also touched by their stories, and he wants to touch the lives of many through his transforming story.

Now we need to mention that no malicious motives were ever proven in Ken's case because only thing he gained from the appalling deeds was a family tragedy and continual agonizing sufferings of his family members. Ken feels that their loved ones should suffer no more because they had done no wrong.

Let us just gleam briefly the stories of the biblical murders. For the record, Moses is attributed in writing the first five books in the

Bible (Genesis, Exodus, Leviticus, Numbers, and Deuteronomy). David wrote most of the Psalms where "The Lord is my shepherd, I shall not be in want"[18] is well-known, memorized, and prayed on by not only the Bible believers, but also the nonbelievers. Paul is incontrovertibly the author of thirteen books in the New Testament of the Bible. They all had malicious motives in murdering innocent human beings, and they all were saved by the grace of their Creator. Likewise, regardless of the motive in question, Ken is also saved by the same grace.

First, the Bible tells the story of angry and hatred Moses, who struck and killed an Egyptian.[19] Moses was enraged when the Egyptian was beating a Hebrew, one of Moses's kind. Then he hid the dead body, assuming nobody had seen the murder. However, Pharaoh, the Egyptian king, found out about the murder and ordered the capture of Moses. Moses then fled from Pharaoh. In this story, Moses's malicious motives were quite clear.

Second, David's story in the Bible likewise shows his malicious motives when he had Uriah, one of his generals and his soldiers, killed in a nonsensical scripted tactical battle scene to cover up David's adulterous affairs with Uriah's wife.[20] Ken's personal letters in the subsequent chapter will share his view on David's story.

Third, Paul's story is the most appalling. His own words, "I persecuted the followers of this Way [Jesus Christ] to their death, arresting both men and women and throwing them into prison."[21] Here we can see that he testified to murdering the followers. The Bible does not say how many followers of Jesus, the Way, were murdered, but we can imagine there could been many.

Paul also testified that his persecuting the followers were severe. He said, "For you have heard of my previous way of life in Judaism, how intensely I persecuted the church of God and tried to destroy

---

[18] Psalms 23:1
[19] Exodus 2:1–15
[20] 2 Samuel 11:15–17
[21] Acts 22:4

it."[22] He really loathed the followers of Jesus. We can observe Paul's condoning the stoning death of Stephen as St. Luke recorded the atrocious stoning. "While they were stoning him [Stephen]...Saul [Paul in Greek] was there giving approval to his death."[23]

In summary, Moses, David, and Paul had malicious motives in taking innocent lives. Moses, in madness, struck an Egyptian and fled in fear of being caught to his own death. David, in an attempt to cover up his adulterous affair with Uriah's wife, had Uriah and his men murdered. Then Paul was running around maniacally, murdering many followers of Jesus. All three had committed atrocious murders with evil motives; however, their lives had been transformed when they answered to God's calling.

Likewise, Ken strongly felt God's calling. Although he had no malicious motives, he admits that the actual deeds were atrocious and inexcusable. However, the state of his insane mind at the time of atrocity was quite dissimilar from the sane minds of Moses, David, and Paul. Regardless, one thing is so true that God can use even the murderers to carry out His redemptive work for the humanity. Ken is answering the divine calling, and this book is a part of answering the call of his Creator God.

---

[22] Galatians 1:13
[23] Acts 7:60 and Acts 8:1

CHAPTER 2

Resume, Job Application

Ken has captured the highlights of his career from his reporting to a boot camp at Fort Knox, Kentucky, on June 13, 1979, just three days after his high school graduation, to the present day in the form of resume titled, "Job Application." From this resume, the reader should gleam what Ken's true devotion has been; that is, the servant-oriented or Christ-like service to the humanity.

Job Application (Ken, The Dreaming Joe, Yi 이강선)

* Position Seeking:
  - Pastor (John 21:15–19), Partnering Strategic Minister (Acts 13:2–3), or Jethro-like Spiritual Advisor (Exodus 18:24)

* Pay: $12.00/month (symbolic) or as ability to give (1 Cor. 16:2) cheerfully (2 Cor. 9:7)
* Duration: Lifetime or by contract. (Birthyear: 1960)
* Duty: Feed and care for God's children and evangelize the lost children through biblical strategic planning for the twenty-first century focused ministries; Assist the church senior leadership, the senior leadership of global-level ministries, and the corporate-level leadership by offering Bible-based visioning, leadership training, team building,

problem solving, accountability, inspiring, and all other leadership skills.

* Background: Was born in Incheon, Korea. Immigrated to USA in 1975. After high school, in 1979, joined the US Army. After serving thirty years in the military, retired in 2009 to Virginia where he had suffered a major mental illness that resulted in his family tragedy in 2010. Ever since then, has been incarcerated. My life story of triumph from tragedy is expected to be published in a book in 2018.
    - The church: since my youth, I have served the church as the president of a Sunday school student body, an acolyte, a greeter, an usher, the treasurer of a church, a choir member, a layman, a deacon, and a hypocrite.

* Education:
    - Doctorate Degree: Candidate for Doctor of Theology, Cypress Bible Institute (CBI, expected completion in 2018)
    - Post-Graduate Degree: MS, National Resource Strategy, Industrial College of Armed Forces, National Defense University
    - Graduate Degrees:
        - MSA, General Administration, Central Michigan University
        - Master of Theology and Master of Divinity, CBI
    - Bachelor Degrees:
        - BS in Computer Science, US Military Academy (West Point)
        - Bachelor of Bible, King's Way School of Ministry

* Credentials:
    - Commissioned and Licensed (US) Minister of Christian gospel, Apostolic Temple Ministries;

Certified Senior Acquisition Professional, US Defense Acquisition University; Certified Information Operation Specialist, Information Resource Management College (US Department of Defense)

* Experience: a thirty-year veteran of US Army (1979–2009) and US Government service (2009–2010), the fifth year (2013–2018) of establishing and running the JoeAnna Ministries (JAM), WWW.JoeAnna.org, and the eighth year (2010–current) of visioning for the Three Joyful Mission Network Centers (Mongolia, Virginia, and tentatively Ohio)
  - Current: Called to serve as Executive Director (JAM), Associate Pastor (Buckingham Christian Fellowship Church), Chaplain (Buckingham Veterans Support Group), Partnering Strategic Minister (New Future and Light of Life Churches, Mongolia), and President (Joyful Mission Network)
  - JoeAnna Ministries (JAM): established in 2013
    - Partnered with Pastor PARK Hi-sook "Anna" (M.Div), established and operated the JAM, a tax-exempt nondenominational charity under section 501(c)(3) of the US Internal Revenue Code;
    - Have ministered unto six Korean-American prisoners in three separate prisons, meeting their emotional and spiritual needs by phone, email, letters, devotional materials, and visits; personally, ministered unto numerous fellow prisoners on site through fellowship, worship, Bible study, counseling, preaching, and sharing the gospel.
    - Have served as Executive Director, JAM, which have provided financial, prayer, and fellowship support to the following:

- Three global level ministries (FamilyLife, Global Mission Ministries, and SEED Ministry International);
- Mongolia Ministries: in association with Pastor Puje Khaltar, the on-site native pastor of New Future Church (needy children) and the Light of Life Church (homeless), have served as his Strategic Pastor performing the duty as so stated in the front;
- Partnered with the Jay & Roxanne Lee missionaries working in the Mongolian International University;
- The LA Skid Row homeless ministry, Christian Broadcast Network (CBN), HeartandSeoul Ministry, US.CTS.TV, SpiritFM.com, The Nature Camp Foundation (Virginia), Fairfax County (Virginia) based ministries (Central Senior Center and Washington Scholarship Foundation), Virginia jail and prison ministries (the Restoration Halfway House by Rehoboth, Salt and Light, ChristSong, Ekklesia Christian Fellowship Church, and Dillwyn First Baptist Church), and Cleveland Korean Presbyterian Church (Ohio).

- US Military and Government Services: Retired as Lieutenant Colonel in 2009
  - Served as Private through Sergeant, Infantry Branch (tactical units); Served as Lieutenant, Captain, and Major, Artillery Branch (tactical and operational units); Served as Major and Lieutenant Colonel, Information System Management Branch (operational and strategic units; Eighth US Army, US Forces Korea, the Republic of Korea/US

Combined Forces Command and US Joint Chiefs of Staff)
- As commissioned artillery officer, commanded an 8" cannon platoon in a nuclear capable battalion (US Army Europe, Germany), liaison for a nuclear-capable Lance missile battery and deactivated the unit in the Korean Peninsula in support of the Denuclearization Treaty, and commanded a Multiple Launch Rocket System and Army Tactical Missile System battery (US Forces Korea)
- Provided classified voice, data, and video wide area network (WAN) connecting over 30 simulation exercise sites (CONUS, Hawaii, Korea, and Japan) and supported six annual four-star level combined and joint (Korea-US) simulated Korean Peninsula Operational Plan (OPLAN) 5027 exercises.
- Provided classified and unclassified computer network systems for the US National Military Command Center (NMCC), Pentagon, and the emergency NMCC Site R at the undisclosed underground bunker; restored and maintained the systems for the senior general officers and their staff after the 9/11 attack at the Pentagon.
- Served as the hand-picked Political and Military Affairs Officer for Korea in J5 Policy and Plans Directorate, the Joint Chiefs of Staff (JCS), Pentagon; Provided the Korean peninsula security policy recommendations working closely with the South Korean Military Attach (Korean Embassy) during the politically sensitive period, 2002–2003, when North Korea's clandestine nuclear program was revealed for the very first time. Briefed the JCS Chairman (four star), the J5 Director (three star),

and the J5 Dep. Dir. for Asia (one star) on Korea security matters
- Served as the certified Systems Synchronization Officer responsible for the $1.2 billion budget to modernize and synchronize the US Army logistics systems and programs in G8 Programs Directorate, US Army Staff, Pentagon; Coordinated with the Congressional Budget Office
- Served as Strategic Planner (GS 14), US National Guard Bureau (strategic corporate level), 2009–2010.

* Decorations: 18 medals and 3 badges
   - Medals: Legion of Merit, Defense Meritorious Service (2), Joint Service Commendation, Army Meritorious Service (3), Army Commendation (3), Army Achievement (3), Army Good Conduct, National Defense Service (2), Global War on Terrorism Service, and Korean Defense Service;
   - Badges: Parachutist, Joint Chiefs of Staff ID, and Army Staff ID

* Life Membership: Association of Graduates (West Point), Association of the US Army, Disabled American Veterans, US Army Historic Foundation, Cleveland Heights High Alumni Foundation, Citizens United for Rehabilitation of Errants, CBN (The 700 Club and the SuperBook), and Spirit FM

CHAPTER 3

Repentance

In the theme of repentance, this author has decided to share Ken's testimonial prison letters to which the reader could humanely relate. Our prayer for you as a reader is that the letters may touch you to bring your heart to repentance as divinely guided before your Creator. These prison epistles should be telling stories from the subject prisoner whom I will refer as "Ken, the Dreaming Joe" from now on. His letters were intended for fellow prisoners, especially Jonathan (Chapter 4), who is charged with a drug-related first-degree murder, and also for all soul-searching readers in the world.

The author hopes that the above paragraph catches the attention of not only you, but also those prisoners serving murder convictions. Every attempt is made to quote exact words from the prison letters with minimum editions to satisfy the publishing requirements. The stories you are about to read are absolutely true stories. This author hopes to stimulate the reader's compassion and empathy toward the storytelling prisoner.

Since 2010 when Ken, the Dreaming Joe, was incarcerated, he had suffered one relapse of the major mental illness in 2014. He wrote "To Whom It May Concern" letter just before he was beginning to enter the relapse. The author wants you to read this letter first, and then another letter about his coming off such horrific relapse of deadly mental illnesses. All subsequent letters are interrelated.

WEST POINTER TO IMPRISONED PREACHER... WHY?

The first letter is Ken, the Dreaming Joe's "hear me out" petition prior to his struggle with the relapse. Then the subsequent letter is a reawakening testimony shared in his JoeAnna Ministries' quarterly message. It was drafted in September 2015 when Ken was about to come off the relapse completely. My prayer is that Ken's testimony grabs your attention to empathize with him, feel his transforming experience, and embrace hope in any hardship or tragedy you might currently facing. Here, the reader should note the dates and years of the two letters.

March 21, 2014

To Whom It May Concern:

> *I am a sinner who does not deserve to live, and yet God continues to pour His saving grace through so many chosen people, especially reconciled family members grieving over the family tragic deaths. Although my offenses are inexcusable, I humbly in contrition beg for your empathy and compassion as you read this letter.*
>
> *My mental health was a significant issue, and yet it was, in my current right state of mind, not properly addressed at my trial. As far as I am concerned, my mental state at the time of offenses should have been the significant factor that was not clearly presented to the jury.*[24] *I did not premediate the unthinkable offenses during those darkest moments. I would like you to consider all medical diagnoses and opinions made by the experts as quoted in the subsequent paragraphs in this letter. I do miss my family so very much, and I want you to*

---

[24] Refer to the Foreword pages in this book to understand the situation better.

know that I did love them very much until the very tragic moments. I had no motives, and no motives were proven at the trial either.

Since my surviving the 9/11 terror attack at the Pentagon in 2001, I had begun receiving mental health treatments and taken medications for the mental illness symptoms until January 2, 2014, when Dr. Rakesh Sood, Licensed Clinical Psychiatrist for the Virginia Department of Corrections, medically released me.[25] Moreover, I have been free from any medication since September 2013.[26] Neither am I having any suicidal, homicidal, or delusional thoughts anymore.[27] Furthermore, I am not suffering from insomnia or any other medical ailments as before.[28] Now I do have strong will to live and serve others.[29]

I like you to consider the following opinions of three mental health treatment professionals: Dr. Thomas Wise, Dr. Jennifer Rasmussen, and Dr. Anita L. Boss:

Dr. Wise, licensed clinical psychiatrist at INOVA Fairfax Hospital, Virginia, opined, "Mr. Yi's most likely diagnosis was major depressive disorder with psychotic features." The doctor also concluded, "Mr. Yi had rammed his head against a

---

[25] Ken sought for the mental health treatment shortly after writing this letter. He was once again cleared from the mental health treatment officially in January 2016.

[26] Ken had to be put back on the same medication in the summer of 2014.

[27] These symptoms, except the homicidal thoughts, had returned after writing this letter.

[28] These symptoms had returned after writing this letter.

[29] This statement might have been written as Ken was desperately seeking the delusional clemency.

wall with such force that he fractured two facets of his cervical vertebrae. If this isn't mental illness, I am not sure what is!"

Dr. Rasmussen, licensed clinical psychologist at Virginia Central State Hospital, was the prosecutor's expert witness. She concluded, "Mr. Yi's depression and suicidal ideation likely contributed to his actions in the alleged offenses. It further seems likely that if his symptoms of depression had been adequately controlled these offenses would not have occurred."

Finally, Dr. Boss, board certified forensic psychologist and licensed clinical psychologist, was my defense expert witness. She concluded, "There is ample evidence to indicate that Mr. Yi was suffering from a severe mental disorder at the time of the alleged offenses." She opined, "At the time of the alleged offenses, Mr. Yi was suffering from a severe mental disease that substantially impaired his ability to appreciate the nature, quality, or wrongfulness of his actions."[30]

Thank you!

Sincerely,
Kenston K. "Joe" Yi

---

[30] Dr. Anita L. Boss's evaluation interview with Ken will be covered in Chapter 11. Ken concurs with her conclusions.

October 10, 2015

Dear God So Loved,[31]

Greetings...long time, no hear! For about ten months, I had thought about fugitive prophets, Elijah and Jonah (1 King 19 and Jonah 1, 4). Both prophets tried to flee away from God and wanted to die instead of carrying out their assigned ministries. While Elijah and Jonah physically attempted to flee from God, such attempt was simply unimaginable for me due to my confinement which only aggravated my anguish.

During this agonizing period, I even stopped answering frequent letters from my own octogenarian parents. No cards for either Christmas or birthday, which was just a glimpse of my agonizing moments. More to come in a book...maybe.

However, unbelievably in past May, an old hymn, "Be not dismayed ♪♫ Whatever betide ♪♪ God will take care of you...Beneath His wings of love abide ♪♫ God will take care of you"[32] *began ringing in my ears like "a gentle whisper"*[33] *Then I started gradually regaining strength physically, mentally, and spiritually.*

Recently, I am joyfully finding myself smiling and socializing more. Once again, I have experienced the mystery of God's doing. Although I do not fully understand His doing, I do trust the Lord. My

---

[31] Quarterly newsletter message was handwritten and so it was uploaded in JoeAnna.Org in October 2015

[32] Agape Publishing Company, Ltd., "Be not dismayed Whate'er Betide by C.D. and W.S. Martin (1904)," (Seoul, Korea, 1997), p. 432.

[33] 1 King 19:12

reawakening is a clear testimony of unwavering prayer support my parents and friends like you have poured upon me. So I do sincerely thank you!

Oh, I am now a Bachelor of Bible, studying to become a Master of Theology. The article New York Times Magazine[34] was going to publish about me is put on hold for now because I sense that the timing is off.[35] Finally, the tax exemption status was granted by both the Virginia State and the Federal IRS.[36]

May God continue to give you peace, His Shalom!

*Slave of Christ Jesus,
Ken, the "Joe"*

---

[34] John Haskins, the *New York Times Magazine* Managing Editor, assigned Ms. Rachel L. Snyder to write an article about the phenomenon of familicide in his letter dated January 27, 2014. Ms. Snyder then contacted Ken and conducted a video-recorded and her handwritten note-taking interviews with him.

[35] Ken eventually decided not to publish the story through the *New York Time Magazine*. As a result of his decision, this book is published.

[36] Ken was talking about the JoeAnna Ministries cofounded with Anna Park. It is a nonprofit charity organization recognized under the US IRS code 501(c)(3) and the Commission of the Commonwealth of Virginia.

CHAPTER 4

Forgiveness
Asking for Mercy!

In this chapter, Ken's letter expresses his being reconciled with the victim's family and, more importantly, his Creator God. The Bible says that every believer and follower of Jesus, the Reconciler, was given the "ministry of reconciliation."[37] Since Jesus has reconciled the sinful humanity with the Creator, the followers of Jesus are also given the same ministry of reconciliation.

Any broken relationships, according to the Bible, can only be renewed when forgiving occurs between the parties having "something against"[38] each other. Jesus teaches us to "be reconciled" to a fellow human being when there is something to be worked out. Ken recognized that he had to be reconciled with the victim's family and his God. So Jesus's teaching was obeyed.

---

[37] 2 Corinthians 5:18
[38] Matthew 5:23–24

WEST POINTER TO IMPRISONED PREACHER... WHY?

September 21, 2016

Dear Jonathan,

Could you please allow me to speak to you as a fellow prisoner? Before I begin, I want to declare that I have never planned for any murder, period.

You know, I have always wanted to name my son, Jonathan, if I ever get one, because this name epitomizes true friendship. Willing to sacrifice his own life and almost assured throne to the nation of Israel, Jonathan had saved his friend David's life multiple times during the pursuits from Jonathan's father, King Saul. Such admirable friendship has so touched myself that I have always wished for a son like Jonathan.

Regardless of our convictions and incarcerations, I do believe that we can be Jonathan-like friends between us and to others who need true friends.

Desiring to be a Jonathan-like friend to you, I want to share my story which could be yours. First, there is absolutely no excuse for the horrible sin I had committed against God and my family. I am a tragic result of a failed familicide attempt. I am talking about taking precious lives of my own wife and adopted daughter. From this horrific tragedy, I have gained nothing but grief. Thus, no motive was ever found or proven because I have none but love for my deceased family.

"How could you?" you may ask, like so many have asked. My answer is very simple. I had always loved my family, and I was suffering from a deadly, uncontrollable mental illness. I am a tragic victim

of the 9/11 terrorist attacks. I am also a veteran who could have perished like forty veterans who had perished waiting to receive the needed health treatments from the failed Veterans Affairs (VA) medical system. "Cheap excuses!" you may cry out thinking that my excuses sound like easy cop-outs. Only God knows!

I ask you to continue reading and give me a benefit of doubt. My story could be your story. Could you believe me if I told you that I committed the horrible killings because I loved my wife and daughter so much? "Huh, love? That's just insane!" you may shout out to me. Of course, to this day, I have pleaded legally "Not Guilty by the Reason of Insanity (NGRI)." To tell my side of the story that the jury did not get to hear in the court, I plan to publish a book later.

Anyhow, let me continue. You would probably agree with me that no sane-minded souls could commit such horrific killings. Only malicious and selfish motives, in my current sane state of mind, could drive sound human beings to kill another being.

Regardless of the state of our minds, what's committed is inexcusable. Fittingly, we need to call it sin. Furthermore, we must come clean before God, the victim's family, and ourselves.

I do not want to dwell in the past too much, so let us look to the future. I do not want to sound preachy to you either, but I came clean by asking for forgiveness from God, my in-law family, and my own loved ones. I am now set free, forgiven, by God's grace and His chosen ones who are my in-law and own family members.

WEST POINTER TO IMPRISONED PREACHER... WHY?

Moreover, I have recommitted my life to my Lord Jesus Christ, whose blood continually cleanses me of all my sins. I am 100 percent convinced that God has never stopped loving you and me even during the tragic dark moments. I am also 100 percent convinced that God wants to use us for his glory. However, we must first come clean before God and the victim's family. Asking for forgiveness to be set free is the first order of business.

Regardless of how and what happened on that tragic day for you and me, God still loves us. Our Creator God can use us as He has used those murderers who wrote the significant portions of the Bible. I enclosed "My Story Is Your Story," which mentions God's using these murderers to write the redemptive story in the Bible.

By God's grace, my partner, Anna Park, and I have found the JoeAnna Ministries (JAM), a non-denominational, nonprofit 501(c)(3) charity organization in 2013. That's almost three years after my lock-up year. We, the JAM, support three globally oriented ministries, five regional prison and jail ministries, and two Korean-American churches to include Washington Scholarship Foundation and Northern Virginia Central Senior Center. We also support four prisoners (Korean-Americans) like you in three prisons. For one prisoner, we provide financial support to pay for his correspondence courses.

We do not just write checks to these supported entities. In addition to the financial support, we provide prayer and fellowship support through letters, phone calls, devotional materials, and visits as necessary. We would like to sponsor you to take the correspondence courses to achieve your academic goals. I do strongly sense that you are highly self-motivated and that you do have strong family support where your minister parents have a ministry of their own serving the needy. Now we are involved, and we look forward to an opportunity to colabor in serving the needy, the hurt, like you and me to give glory to God, the only deserving One. Thank you for your time. God loves you, and so do I!

Your Friend,
Ken, the Joe

Enclosed:
-"My Story is Your Story"[39]
-New York Times Magazine stuff[40]

---

[39] Next chapter tells this story.
[40] John Haskins, managing editor of the *New York Times Magazine*, certified Rachel L. Snyder to write an article about the phenomenon of familicide.

CHAPTER 5

My Story Is Your Story![41]

November 2012, at the time of Ken's sentencing.

I want to talk about my personal tragedy that occurred as a result of my suffering from severe delusional depression and insomnia. Before I begin my story, I want to set the stage so the reader can better understand me.

Tragedies occur every day in life. No family is immune from them. Although we do not fully understand all circumstances surrounding tragedies, we do get blessed (benefited) when we trust sovereign God, who is in full control of *everything*.

Recently, the media got excited about the tragic suicide of Matthew Warren, who was suffering from "deep depression" from his birth as his father explained. Why was this tragedy so attractive to the media when an alarming high rate of suicide continues in the world?[42] Matthew's father is Pastor Rick Warren, who is well-known for his world's best-selling Christian book, *The Purpose Driven Life* which is sold more than thirty million copies.

---

[41] Ken, the Joe, drafted this story in his jail cell, the Fairfax Adult Detention Center, Virginia, in 2012, just two years into his incarceration. At that time, he was unable to be forthcoming to discuss his family tragedy specifically.

[42] This alarming global suicide rate is a common knowledge as reported by the media.

Pastor Warren also leads one of largest churches in the world. His church has more than thirty thousand members. He often gets invited to major TV networks to share his Christian views regarding controversial societal issues such as same-sex marriage and gun control. I mention Pastor Warren's family tragedy to reiterate my point that it can happen to any family. Only those who have suffered from suicidal depression or "deep depression," in my mind, can truly understand the sensitive nature of such deadly mental illness.

I want to share one more factoid before sharing my tragedy. Last year, I took a keen interest in a well-researched *Time* magazine article that reported how the American military continues struggling with the increasing rate of suicides whose major cause is researched as depression, a serious mental disease.[43] Nation's leaders are calling for the change in mind-set in dealing with this illness and to revolutionizing the care and treatment for such disease. The article surprised me by reporting that the military community is experiencing suicides every ninety seconds.[44] It is a really telling story.

Now let me turn to my story. Please pardon me for not getting too much into details of my tragedy. I will share just enough to point out that this mental illness can occur in any family and that such illness must be cared for and treated rightly and timely.

---

[43] Unable to find this article at the time of this writing in 2017. It is assumed that the *Time* reported this in 2011. However, *USA Today* reported on July 1, 2016, "A 2010 calculation by the VA estimates that 22 veterans kill themselves each day. The VA, which has not updated that estimate, says the hotline 'rescues' 30 veterans from suicide each day."

[44] More recently in January/February 2017 Issue of *Disable American Veterans (DAV) Magazine*, Charity Edgar wrote an article, "20 TOO MANY," that the Department of Veterans Affairs examined more than 55 million nationwide records from 1979 to 2014 and found that "an average of 20 veterans die by suicide each day."

WEST POINTER TO IMPRISONED PREACHER... WHY?

I had attempted to take my own life[45] while I was suffering from severe depression. The mental diagnosis is termed as severe delusional depression complicated with an extended period of insomnia and anxiety. I could have been dead or quadriplegic as my surgeon solemnly reminded me, but am now alive with two small bolts holding my broken neck bone and multiple deep scars on my (top) head. Another surgical scar is visible on my neck.

These bolts and scars are distinct reminders that God has a purpose for my staying alive and healthy. I strongly sense and believe that God is calling me into His full-time ministry, and I have decided to obey the calling and prepare myself for God's timing for His mission field for me to follow the Lord's Great Commission.

I have been incarcerated since the summer of 2010, when my family's grievous and unthinkable tragedy occurred.[46] As the book of Job reminds us, nothing in this world, even Satan (I hate this evil in that I hesitate to recognize the evil spirit with a capital "S"), can operate without God's will, plan, purpose, approval, and sovereignty. Pastor Warren stated in *The Purpose Driven Life*, "Everything that happens to a child of God is Father-filtered."[47]

Although believing that my family tragedy and incarceration are so-called God "Father-filtered" is very hard, I have accepted the fact that God has always been in absolute control of my entire life. I strongly believe that my staying alive and healthy has a divine purpose. In this regard, I have willingly decided to be driven by such honorable purpose.

In my strong view, my tragic story could be your own story. I sense in my spirit that such tragic story could end in triumph as

---

[45] This is the third attempt. Multiple hanging attempts had failed. Taking thirteen to fifteen prescribed Ambien pills got him to ER. Another book is expected to cover the details of these suicidal attempts.

[46] This was a failed familicide attempt unfolded in the dark morning on June 13, 2010. The writer at the time of this letter writing could not describe the horrible moments.

[47] Rick Warren, *The Purpose Driven Life* (Grand Rapid, 2002), p.224.

many tragic stories in the Bible show us the transformational truth. The Holy Bible is full of triumphal stories that remind us to be hopeful in the midst of tragedies. Let me just point out Matthew 1:1–6 where the genealogy of Lord Jesus Christ lists several characters who had overcome their respective tragic adversities, and yet God had used them to fulfill His plan of salvation. King David is one clear example besides Tamar, Rahab, Ruth, and Bathsheba. I want to talk about David, whom God called "a man after His own heart"[48] and "a man after my own heart."[49]

Even the secular world is touched by the much writings of King David in the book of Psalms. The Twenty-Third Psalm, "The Lord is my shepherd..."[50] is memorized and recited by many media and public forums, both the Christian and secular communities, as one of inspirational poetic writings. However, the genealogy of Jesus turns ugly when it mentions "David was the father of Solomon, whose mother had been Uriah's wife."[51] Very interesting, isn't it? Wow! We instantly recognize that something is not right in this picture. The genealogy shows that Solomon did not come from David's own wife, and to cover up his adulterous sin, David had Uriah and his soldiers murdered in battle.[52]

How could God use sinful people like David to bring about the Savior Jesus Christ? God is "I AM Who I AM."[53] He is Almighty, and El-Shaddai God can use sinful people, the very unlikely choices, saved by His grace anytime for His own good, His divine purpose. Genesis 50:20 and Romans 8:28 speak of such quintessence of our true God.

I certainly do not often understand God's doing, but I trust His sovereign control of *all* affairs in the world. Like David's tragic

---

[48] 1 Samuel 13:14
[49] Acts 13:22
[50] Psalm 23:1
[51] Matthew 1:6b
[52] 2 Samuel 11:14–17
[53] Exodus 3:14

WEST POINTER TO IMPRISONED PREACHER... WHY?

story which was transformed into the glorious plan of salvation for the humanity, my story, in my strong belief, is yet to be climaxed for God's glory. My story could be your story, and I do pray that we all humbly seek God's face in every circumstance, the good, the bad, and the ugly, and continue to trust Him to fulfill His divine purposes.

Thank you for reading my story, and may God richly bless you. Amen!

Ken Yi
Fairfax County Jail 2012

CHAPTER 6

Hope
A Second Chance!

Here is the petition cover letter Ken has been working on for few years since the victim's family notarized their petition to the Governor of Virginia to pardon Ken. The online petition site, JoeAnna.org/petition, is established for the reader who believes in redemption to support Ken's plea. This chapter will only share the cover letter and all supporting enclosures are available on the petition site. Ken is asking for a second chance to continue doing what he does best: serve the fellow humanity.

April 11, 2017

Minister Kenston K. Yi (#1445347)
Buckingham Correctional Center,
P.O. Box 430, Dillwyn, VA 23936

Governor of Virginia
1111 Broad St, Third Floor
Richmond, VA 23219

Re: Petition for Conditional Pardon – A Second Chance

WEST POINTER TO IMPRISONED PREACHER... WHY?

Dear Honorable Governor:

As a "corrected" prisoner, I humbly petition your pardon because I still plead "Not Guilty by the Reason of Insanity" and no malicious motives were evident or proven.

Besides, your Assist AG Eugene Murphy was apologetic for the current law was not favorable for my case in which major mental illnesses got lost as the core focuses (Encl. A). Anyhow, my Mental Health Level has been downgraded to 0 from the suicidal watch at the 2010 arrest.

Moreover, the victim's family (my forgiving mother-in-law) has waited patiently for the outcome of their petition for my pardon in 2014 (Encl. B). Ultimately, my compassionate eighty-two-year-old mother-in-law, eighty-three-year-old father, and eighty-two-year-old mother should suffer no more from pitiful emotional shackles for they have done no wrong, deserving of such misery.

Furthermore, I was during my incarceration commissioned and licensed as a minister (Encl. C) by earning three degrees (Encl. D) and still selflessly serving (Encl. E). Such devotion to serve others is in keeping with thirty-one years of honorable service in the US Military (1979–2009) retiring as Lt. Colonel (Encl. F) and in the National Guard Bureau (2009–2010) until the major aggravating illness led to a failed familicide attempt (Encl. G) which got me incarcerated.

Overcoming all odds as a fifteen-year-old immigrant, I became a commissioned West Point officer rising from the enlisted rank and earned eighteen medals where prestigious Legion of Merit *is the highest (Encl. F). Despite my long loyal service to the nation, the Dept. of Veterans Affairs (VA) had disappointed and failed to provide me with adequate and timely treatment for Survivor Guilt and Post-Traumatic Stress Disorder sustained after surviving the 9/11 attack at the Pentagon. At last, I had tried hard to battle these lethal mental illnesses during my thorny transition to civilian life but gotten tragically tangled up in the middle of the perpetual VA controversy.*

In short, my worthy service to the nation, genuine academic achievements, exemplary resume (Encl. H), positive references reflecting continued selfless service (Encl. I), and flawless prison record (Encl. J) hopefully inspire you to pardon me. Offering no excuses and seeking no sympathy, I do humbly plead for your empathy, benefit of doubt, and mercy.

Thank you,

Kenston K. "the Joe" Yi
Lt. Colonel (Ret.), US Army

CHAPTER 7

Why Jesus?

Once again, the reader is reminded that the purpose of this book is not to Christianize anyone. Since Ken has found hope in the Christian faith, exposing the reader to who Christ, the Way, is necessary.

Therefore, this chapter will share the following:

1) Who Is the Father of the Baby?
2) What Calling in Prison?
3) Answering the Calling in Jerusalem?

May the Way become clear to the reader to understand the faith that gives Ken the hope!
(Acts 9:2; 19:9; 9:23; 22:4; 24:14; and 24:22)

Who Is the Father of the Baby?

This message was written for the 2016 Christmas season. The reader is reminded that this book's purpose is not an attempt to Christianize anyone but to share Ken's faith in Christianity. Without Jesus Christ, there would not be the Christian faith. So the reader should understand this Jesus to whom Ken lost his energy, mind, heart, and soul. Jesus still makes significant impact in people's lives today after two thousand years of His death, resurrection, and ascension according to the four gospels.[54]

"I'm pregnant…three months already!"
"Say again? Remember our holy matrimony? Who slept with you?"
"I'm still a virgin. My purity will always be there for you!"
"Are ya insane? Who is the father of the baby?"
"God is…the baby is to be called holy!"
"Holy? C'mon…I just can't take it anymore!"
"Remember Isaiah? The baby is the long-waited Messiah!"
"Gimme a break! The matrimony needs to be called off…very quietly!"
"Remember Malachi? The baby is the rising sun of righteousness!"
"Are ya insane, Mary? I can't take you in…you can't be my wife…sorry!"
"Please, Joseph…open your heart and hear the voice of God. Come to me!"

About seven hundred years before such suspense, Prophet Isaiah uttered, "The virgin will be with child and will give birth to a son, and will call him Immanuel" (Is. 7:14).

St. Matthew (a converted Jewish tax collector) later quoted Isaiah's exact words and exclaimed that "Immanuel means God with

---
[54] The Gospels of Matthew, Mark, Luke, and John in the Bible.

us" (Matt. 1:23). He also wrote, "Joseph was a righteous man and did not want Mary exposed to public disgrace." Thinking Mary cheated on him, Joseph decided "to divorce her quietly" (Matt. 1:19).

About four hundred years before the looming divorce, Prophet Malachi foretold, "The Sun of righteousness will rise with healing in its wings" (Mal. 4:2). This prophecy according to St. Luke (a converted Greek physician) was fulfilled by the baby in Mary's womb. After thorough interviews and investigations (Lk. 1:1–4), Luke recorded that the rising Sun has come from heaven to shine on those living in darkness and in the shadow of death (Lk.1:78–79).

Ultimately, a divine wake-up call (Matt. 1:24) reaffirmed Joseph of God's promised redemptive seed coming from his lineage, King David (2 Chr. 6:16–17).

"Joseph, son of David…take Mary…as your wife…the baby conceived in her is from the Holy Spirit…name him Jesus because he will save his people from their sins." (Matt. 1:23)

Christmas is about this Jesus. During this Christmas holiday season, may our hearts hear "the sounding joy…Repeat…Repeat…The Lord is come!" (I. Watts 1719 & G.F. Händel 1742)

PENUEL KODESH

What Calling in Prison?

March 30, 2017

Dear God So Loved,

Regardless of anyone's feeling, Trump is now called the president of the USA. Somewhat similarly, I am now called Rev., Minister, Pastor, Chaplain, or Mok-Sa-Nym (Korean for the formers). Needing no justification for such calling, many encouragers have touched my heart; i.e., Chaplain Ron Baker's words stand out, "If God calls one…if God has ordained you that is all that is necessary." I joyfully exclaim, "Amen!"

Living up to such holy calling, I do often ask our Father in heaven to empower us to carry out Jesus's commission (Acts 1:8). My "Jerusalem" is the prison here where caring and feeding God's children, preaching and sharing the gospel, overseeing the corporate worship and Bible study and the Veterans POD church, enjoying the fellowship and discipleship, and much more do continue.

Then with all our supported partners, we cover all Judea, and Samaria, and the ends of the earth. They are FamilyLife, Global Mission Ministries, and SEED Ministry Int'l serving globally, three native Mongolian churches (New Future, Light of Life, Open Fellowship of the Mongolian Int'l Univ.), four broadcast networks (CBN, CTS, Spirit FM, and HeartandSeoul Ministry), Virginia-based jail and prison ministries (Rehoboth, Salt and Light, Dillwyn First Baptist Church, and Ekklesia Christian Fellowship), ChristSong Ministry serving other state prisons, Potters House serving the LA Skid Row homeless, Virginia-based charities (Central Senior Center, Washington Scholarship Foundation, and Clifton Korean Baptist Church), and the Cleveland Korean Presbyterian Church (Ohio).

So by the Lord's leading and providing resources and with your fellowship and prayer support extending beyond just receiving monetary donations, our mission faithfully continues: "By empowerment of the Holy Spirit and our thanksgiving to Everlasting Father, proactively serve the hurt to glorify only Mighty God!" Amen!

Joyfully in Jesus,
Ken, the Dreaming Joe, with Anna

Answering the Calling in Jerusalem?

Here is a selection of nine email testimonies and one deep concerning email Ken sent to his Sunday school pastor, Rev. Dr. LEE Byung-hee (President, Global Mission Ministries). The last email shows Ken's unrelenting apologetic confrontation with (or a godly rebuking of) his mentor pastor in defense of the gospel.

Jpay.com has installed a KIOSK machine in each POD where 64 prisoners cohabit. One of the KIOSK features is the email which costs one e-stamp to send one email. Each stamp costs between 25 and 45 cents depending on the quantity of purchase. Although limited in functions, KIOSK has been a blessing for Ken to e-communicate with his ministry partners all the way to Mongolia.

The term "Mok-Sa-Nym" means pastor in Korean.

From: Kenston Yi
Date: 7/24/2016
To: Byung Hee Lee

Hello Mok-Sa-Nym,

Hope this email finds you well in Christ, even during such scorching heat waves.

Here we have no AC. The POD hall registers between 84 to 86 degrees with two commercial wall fans, a residential ceiling fan, and an 8-inch desktop fan per person in each two-man cell. Thank God that I also learned to be content in Christ like Apostle Paul declared. Amen!

I'm currently finishing the theme's research papers (sixty pages minimum). The ten-page paper on "Jesus in Hell?" was graded A+ with the help of the Holy Spirit and Anna. Your feedback is also

WEST POINTER TO IMPRISONED PREACHER... WHY?

mentioned in the paper, and I hope to get the paper uploaded on our website soon. Writing and editing the paper is challenging but manageable. I should be done with the Th.M program by this September.

Then I will begin the study to earn the M.Div program that the Cypress Bible Institute has added. So I thanked the Pilgrims Theology Seminary for their trying to accommodate me with the developing a master's program and let them know that I have signed for the M.Div program with the institute. With the Th.M courses I have taken, I only need to finish just twelve courses to earn the M.Div degree. I hope to get it done within a year.

Ref. the minister General License, I was glad that I would not be binding denominationally when my application for the license is accepted and processed. I plan to send the application with the final paper for the Th.M. I would still like to hear how you view this license. I'm also interested in how the Korean Christian community views about the minister license.

I am told that the license is recognized by the hospital, the jail/prison, etc. Will be authorized to preach, baptize, administer communion, etc.

Just curious. Thank you!

Cheers in Christ,
Ken

PENUEL KODESH

From: Kenston Yi
Date: 9/22/2016
To: Byung Hee Lee

Hello Mok-Sa-Nym!
Praise the Lord. Hallelujah.

Just mailed you the letter written for Jonathan. This letter writing took me back to 2012 in the Fairfax ga-mok (Jail) where I drafted a four-page testimony titled "My Story Is Your Story." It is still just a draft, and I had asked only four people to comment on it. I never got to finish the story.

This letter-writing experience had me wiping tears, blowing my nose, and missing my beloved family. Still do not understand why, but I choose to trust the Lord with Gen. 50:20 and Rom. 8:28.

I strongly sense that God wants me to use Jonathan, but I wonder if God wants to crush his soul more. I ask the Holy Spirit to touch Jonathan's heart and use my letter to turn his heart to God.

Mok-Sa-Nym, I'm 100 percent convinced, unless Jonathan comes to the realization like the prodigal son in Luke, that he has committed a horrible sin before God and the victim's family regardless of his mental state or the drug excuse, God will not use him.

His life will be incredibly transformed when he utters, "I am sorry," and asks for forgiveness. We cannot play the Adam-Eve game with God.

May God bless our souls for His glory!

Thank you for the opportunity to minister unto Jonathan.

Cheers in Christ,
Ken

WEST POINTER TO IMPRISONED PREACHER... WHY?

From: Kenston Yi
Date: 9/23/2016
To: Byung Hee Lee

Good morning Mok-Sa-Nym,

Hallelujah!
It is strange that the Holy Spirit seems to stir up my spirit in tears and runny nose frequently after writing the letter to Jonathan. I thank God because I'm going through the healing process. I'm very confident that I will continue to be more than a conqueror in Christ. Please continue to pray for me. Amen!

The last paper for the Th.M is mailed out. For the practicum purposes, I would like to ask you to send an email to Chancellor D. R. Vestal, Ph.D.

I would appreciate your email if you mentioned the following:

1. *How long you have known me.*
2. *How I have helped you in your ministries?*
3. *Etc.*

Thank you!

Cheers in Christ,
Ken

PENUEL KODESH

From: Kenston Yi
Date: 11/5/2016
To Byung Hee Lee
Growing seed you have planted in me…

Hi, Mok-Sa-Nym,

Hallelujah!
Thank you for your quick response.
We should be back to normal starting this Monday, and I should be able to call you on November 8. Just in case, I would like to begin dialing, starting at 7:30 a.m. your time because we normally get inside for count 11:00–12:00 daily. Evening hours are available too but noisier, 5–6 p.m. your time.

Since last Friday, we are being let out one hour each a.m., p.m., and evening for shower, phone, kiosk, and indoor pod recreation. This happens every quarter for about a week. It started last Monday. Today is the sixth day.

I am at true peace. You know, Mok-Sa-Nym, unless one experiences this peace that God gives and that surpasses all understanding (Phil 4), it just cannot be explained. It needs to be experienced. Hallelujah!
Mok-Sa-Nym, I am a growing seed you have planted back in the '70s. You have confirmed and baptized me in Jesus Christ. Now you are about to give me your blessing in Jesus Christ's name. I am just cheerful about it.
Just desiring to make you comfortable, giving me your verbal blessing in the Lord's name, I like to share the citation on the certificate.

WEST POINTER TO IMPRISONED PREACHER... WHY?

"This is to certify that, having been called of the Lord Jesus Christ to preach the Gospel, Kenston K Yi is hereby commissioned as a Minster of the Gospel to fulfill that call of God and authorized with State, Provincial, and International Laws so long as his life and teaching is consistent with the Word of God, and the By-laws of and statements of faith, and fellowship of this organization."

Signed by Bishop, Pastor, and Secretary
Sealed by Apostolic Temple Ministries
Endorsed by Shema Israel Christian Ministries International

I share this with you because I am 100 percent convinced that I am now entitled to a God-given "Minister," a humble title. So I need to be called as God has called me regardless of anyone's opinions.

So I would like to ask you as I have asked my family members, friends, and fellow children of God. Could you please call me "Minister Ken" in English until you can comfortably call me "Mok-Sa" in Korean?

I do not wish to be like the ones who go through a fancy ordination ceremony and then leave the church with the "Mok- Sa" title. There are no obligations at all. This is a sad story.

Thank you for your understanding and prayers.

Cheerfully in Christ,
Ken

PENUEL KODESH

From: Kenston Yi
Date: 11/6/2016
To: Byung Hee Lee
Fasting and praying for three days…

Hallelujah Mok-Sa-Nym!

I have decided to fast and pray for three days. I am compelled to sacrifice myself to the Lord for two reasons.

1. *The presidential election, I have shared my views on this with you. I pray that your family voted for the Bible principles.*
2. *Verbal blessing this week.*

First, I have received the parental verbal blessing this morning during our daily devotion using Gen. 48:15–16.

Second, I am about to receive the authoritative verbal blessing from Bishop Vestal. I have asked him to verbalize the commissioning me as a minister. I would like to hear the blessing of the citation on the certificate verbalized.

Third, I am about to receive your inspirational blessing as a mentor. As I prayed on my knees this morning, I have come to John 17:6–19. To help prepare for the blessing, I am drafting this email and sharing some facts about my getting out of Gam-ok (Jail).

Fourth, I am receiving solidarity verbal blessings from Godly ministers and colaborers in Christ. I felt that God has directed me to John 17:20–26 for this blessing.

WEST POINTER TO IMPRISONED PREACHER... WHY?

Fifth, I will also be receiving friendly blessings from my long-time friends. I also felt that God has directed me to John 13:34–35.

Mok-Sa-Nym, I am a nondenominational minister who asked the Bishop that I desire not to be bonded to any denominations. I only desire to be bonded to our Master Jesus Christ. I want to remain a bond-servant, doulos slave of Christ.

Having been praying for God's will for getting out of Gam-ok Jail using Malachi 4:2, I would like to share the following facts for you to consider as you prepare for the blessing on me.

Governor's clemency[55]: by the stroke of his pen, I can be out any day. Although my in-laws have documented the petition for my pardon back in 2014, I wanted the petition to be held until the right timing. We can submit the clemency packet every two years. We are shooting for next year to do so

I am certain God will someday let me out.

Cheerfully in Christ,
Ken

---

[55] Geriatric Conditional Release: Ken is entitled for this program, an annual parole board, starting in 2020. It's only a few years away.

PENUEL KODESH

From: Kenston Yi
Date: 11/8/2016
To: Byung Hee Lee

Hello Mok-Sa-Nym,

 Thank you so much for your blessing. It means so much to me. Your blessing touched the hearts of my parents and mine definitely!
 I could not hold blowing by runny nose and flowing tears. I tried not to disturb my bunkmate, but it went on for the whole sixty minutes of praying during the lunch hour count-time.
 God does work wonders. Thank you so much!

Cheerfully in Christ,
Ken

WEST POINTER TO IMPRISONED PREACHER... WHY?

From: Kenston Yi
Date: 11/15/2016
To: Byung Hee Lee
Ref Pastor David Kim...
Hi Mok-Sa-Nym!
Hallelujah!

Would like to share a simple testimony and prayer request please before I talk about Kim Mok-Sa-Nym.

Here a number of fellow prisoners do not get to go to the funerals to see their loved ones buried. One good friend here fell into this case. His dad passed away, and he has been in grief because he is unable to go home to see his family. As I was comforting him with my hand on his shoulder, I strongly sensed why God has me here.

Now as a card-carrying minister, I am more confident to minster unto the emotionally troubled and spiritually challenged. I thanked God for this opportunity in tears.

On November 18 (between 9:10 a.m. to 9:30 a.m.), I will deliver a speech at the graduation ceremony. It is a short message of inspiration and hope. With Anna, I discussed having it uploaded onto our page someday. She will be here for the ceremony. God seems to get me running. I was planning on going slow humbly, but I am in the hands of Almighty Father God. Could you please remember me then to pray for me? I will keep you informed.

Elder Dr. Lee, Sang Jun, gave me his verbal blessing. So did Deacon Tony Hahn. So did Pastor Steve Hong (Kyung-nam) and more.

Agape,
Ken

PENUEL KODESH

From: Kenston Yi
Date: 11/18/2016
To: Byung Hee Lee
The graduation ceremony

Hallelujah Mok-Sa-Nym!

Thank you for your prayer! Here is another testimony that is too good to be shared with just you and your lovely wife Mok-Sa-Nym. Could it be printed in the Gospel paper of which she is a reporter? I will soon have pictures and the prepared speech uploaded on our webpage.

I felt the Holy Spirit working to manifest Himself during my speech (prepared for a four-minute speech but ended up being a fifteen-minute one) and throughout the ceremony attended by more than 150 people. It was just awesome!

I did not even plan or think about saying the last two statements during the unwritten introduction, but my utterance of these words can only be attributed to the Holy Spirit.

"There were few things changed from 1979 when I last wore the yellow tassel at the Cleveland Heights High. Its color was black and yellow symbolizing tiger. Since then my hair has gotten grayer, bifocals, two root canals, and four fillings in my mouth, but one thing has not changed. I am still handsome (got some laughs. Up to this point was planned.) You know I must say as I earned the master's degree in theology, God is also still alive and well."

These last two statements can only be thought of as impromptu words of the Holy Spirit. Anyhow,

WEST POINTER TO IMPRISONED PREACHER... WHY?

all above statements are not part of my prepared speech.

Yes, God is still alive and well. I felt such presence at the ceremony. I would like you to see the full prepared text and consider sharing it with the readers of the newspaper. My message was for the whole world anyhow. [see the last pages of the book]

Thank you again.

Cheerfully in Christ,
Ken

PENUEL KODESH

From: Kenston Yi
Date: 12/7/2016
To: Byung Hee Lee
A testimony this wonderful morning…

Hallelujah Mok-Sa-Nym!

I started to raise my right hand and give a daily morning blessing to the correctional officers (Gan-su) whenever two or more come around each cell daily to count the heads. I declared, "Receive the blessing in the Name of Jesus Christ!" Then one of the two gave me a big smile.

The grace, the blessing, in Jesus is available as a gift, but one has to receive it. The hearer of the good news, the blessing, in Jesus has to accept it. Glory be to God!

Then I prayed with my cellmate this morning, prophesizing that Artee, a skeptic pod-mate, when he gets out in two years, will be a great preacher of the gospel. I told Randy, my roommate, that God gave me that revelation whether anyone believes it or not.

Then I walked over to Artee and sat down to share that revelation. I declared, "Artee, you know what? Whether you believe it or not, I have the revelation from God that you will be a great preacher of the gospel when you get out in two years. I will be watching you!"

Then I shared a story about another skeptic who said we came from the air, not God, became a Sunday school teacher. This skeptic was my chemistry tutor.

WEST POINTER TO IMPRISONED PREACHER... WHY?

Regardless of my standing up for God or not during the tutoring sessions, I do believe God can transform anyone to preach the gospel of Jesus Christ. I assured Artee that Apostle Paul and I once were skeptics like he is now, but God changed Paul and me to preach the gospel. I reminded Artee that God can also change him. Surprisingly, Artee said, "Thank you! I really appreciate that!" I even told him that God may use him to partner with the JoeAnna Ministries whose Christmas message was given to him last night.

Wow, I am so joyful this morning!

God is so good! Immanuel, Hallelujah!

Cheers in Christ,
Ken

PENUEL KODESH

From: Kenston Yi
Date: 1/3/2018
To: Byung Hee Lee
Subject: Preaching the Word (Acts 2:4) as so written by the Holy Spirit

Hi Mok-Sa-Nym,

Happy New Year to your lovely family!

Although I do respect you and your wife Mok-Sa-Nym, I must obey the calling of Lord Jesus to defend His gospel.

I humbly declare that regardless of our personal views on Acts 2:4, we must not alter the exact written word of God. I sensed the leading of the Holy Spirit to 2 Tim. 3:16-4:5. In these verses, the Word commands us to preach the Word, not our opinions.

Your preaching Acts 2:4 deleting the word, "filled" as the Holy Spirit inspired St. Luke to write is a heresy which I will expose in my next book. This email will be strongly considered as the "After Thought" epilogue of my 1st book.

May the Holy Spirit keep all of us filled to obey the Word of God! Nobody...neither the Pope nor Billy Graham can alter the written word period. Amen? Amen!!!

Immanuel,
Ken, the Joe, Yi

Theological Writings of Ken

    The following three chapters could be controversial to some Bible students, theologians, pastors, and teachers. Some may find Ken's writings beneficial because they are based on the scriptures. Ever since Ken began the walk in Christina faith, the topics of Jesus being in hell, the Sabbath, and tithing have troubled him. He never dared asking questions about them. But as Ken began studying theology and divinity, in his mind, he has found the truth in those controversial topics. The author feels that these writings serve the purpose of this book. The reader should find the chapters very interesting.

    May God bless your readings of the Holy Words!

CHAPTER 8

Oh, Jesus Was Never in Hell!

Apostles' Creed

"I believe in God the Father Almighty, maker of Heaven and earth, and in Jesus Christ, his Only Son our Lord, who was conceived by the Holy Ghost, born of the Virgin Mary, suffered under Pontius Pilate, was crucified, dead, and buried; <u>He descended into hell</u>; The third day he rose again from the dead; He ascended into heaven, And sitteth on the right hand of God the Father Almighty; from thence He shall come to judge the quick and the dead. I believe in The Holy Ghost, The Holy Catholic Church, the Communion of Saints, The forgiveness of sins, The resurrection of the body. And the life everlasting. Amen."

An old friend exclaimed, "Nobody will go to hell because a loving God would not send any of His created humans to the eternal punishment to be burned in hell fire forever." As a baby Christian, I quietly and intensely listened to the highly opinionated friend. Actually, the very concept of hell has baffled my mind since long before such encounter of the universal salvation theology. After I became a Christian, and whenever I recited the Apostles' Creed, I was very much bothered and intrigued by the words in the Creed, "He descended into hell." In this paper, I want to unequivocally assert that Jesus never went to such horrible place called hell.

WEST POINTER TO IMPRISONED PREACHER... WHY?

Since my youth, one thing has been very clear that I would never want to be in hell. Likewise, I would not want anyone to end up there either. As a theology student, I have studied the "Jesus in Hell?" course from the Cypress Bible Institute (CBI) and the writings of other Bible scholars on the same question. Then I have unequivocally concluded that the eternal Hell, "the lake of fire,"[56] the place for the unredeemed, does exist and that Jesus Christ, the Redeemer, has never gone to this hell.

Although the CBI course offered two different views on the question of Jesus going to hell after his death on the cross, I find both views presented respectively by Dr. Gary D. Landers and Dr. Donald R. Vestal as one view which supports my theme. Here I also want to dispel any theory that Jesus went to the hell. My Lord Jesus had no divine reasons for being in such place of internal torment designated for the unrighteous. In my view, the true Gospel of Jesus Christ is for the lost sheep on earth, not anywhere else, and certainly the hell is not for the Gospel at all.

First, I want to define what hell is using the words of Jesus Christ because we are talking about whether He went to that place or not. Then I want to present my researched writings to support my theme. Before I proceed, I want to express my unspeakable joy in knowing that I am not alone in believing that our Lord and Savior Jesus never went to hell. I am also delighted to address my continual question in the Apostle's Creed, "He descended into hell."[57]

When Jesus was speaking to His disciples before He sent them out two by two to preach the kingdom of heaven in Matthew (Matt) 10, Jesus undoubtedly spoke Aramaic. Zondervan Compact Bible Dictionary points out, "It is probably safe to assert that our Lord habitually spoke Aramaic and Greek."[58] Since Jesus was

---

[56] Revelation 20:14
[57] Agape Publishing Company, Ltd., The NIV Korean-American Explanation Bible, (Seoul, 2003), the front cover insert.
[58] Zondervan, Zondervan's Compact Bible Dictionary, (Grand Rapid, 1993), p.51.

speaking to His Hebrew disciples, He could not have spoken in Greek. However, the original Greek text in Matt. 10:28 is written as "Gehenna." This Greek word is also used to describe a valley called "Hinnom" in Joshua 15:8 and Nehemiah 11:30. Zondervan states, "After the OT period, Jewish apocalyptic writers began to call the Valley of Hinnom the entrance to hell, later hell itself. The word occurs 12 times in the NT, always translated Hell ASV, RSV margin 'Gehenna.' Eleven times it is on the lips of Jesus; as the final punishment."[59]

In the context of Jesus's commissioning His disciples in Matt.10, I believe Matthew meant Jesus's word, "Gehenna," as a place for "the final punishment," not a geographic location, the Valley of Hinnom. Moreover, Matthew, Mark, and Luke recorded Jesus using the same Greek word, Gehenna, to describe being cast into hell (Gehenna).

Matt. 5:22 and Mark 9:47 quote Jesus's words, "Cast into hell (Gehenna) fire" while Luke 12:5 quotes, "Cast into hell (Gehenna)." Here I like to share how Holman Illustrated Bible Dictionary defines hell:

Hell: Usually understood as the final abode of the unrighteous dead wherein the ungodly suffer eternal punishment; the term translates one OT word and several NT words.

Old Testament Usage: The only Hebrew word translated hell in the KJV (though not in modern translations) is Sheol. Sheol itself is a broad term that, depending on the context, may signify the abode of both the righteous dead and the ungodly dead.

New Testament Usage: In the NT three words are translated hell:

- Gehenna (Matt.5:22, 29–30; 10:28; 18:19; Mark 9:43, 45, 47; Luke 12:5; James 3:6)

---

[59] Ibid., p.191.

WEST POINTER TO IMPRISONED PREACHER... WHY?

- Hades (Matt.11:23; 16:18; Luke 10:15; 16:23; Acts 2:27, 31; Revelation 1:18; 20:13–14)
- Tartarus (2 Peter 2:4)[60]

Holman Dictionary continues, "It is significant that, contrary to Sheol, none of the NT terms for hell or Gehenna are used simply for the grave. There is fundamental difference between Hades and Gehenna that is vital to the understanding of God's punitive justice. From its use in the NT, Hades is viewed as the place that receives the ungodly for the intervening period between death and resurrection. Gehenna may be equated with the everlasting fire that was originally prepared for the devil and his angels (Matt. 25:41), and the lake of fire in Rev. 20:14, into which are cast death and hell. Following the resurrection and the judgment of the lost, Gehenna becomes the final place of punishment by eternal fire."[61]

Among the four words (Sheol, Hades, Gehenna, and Tartarus) as Holman explains from where the English word "hell" might have come, I find that Jesus had probably used the Hebrew word, "Sheol," in Matt. 5:22 when He was conversing with His Hebrew speaking disciples and natives. Then when the Gospels were written in Greek, the "sheol" was probably translated as "Gehenna." Regardless of whether "Sheol" or "Gehenna" was used, Jesus was talking about a place of eternal judgment.

As Holman further explains such eternal judgment as God's punitive justice and everlasting punishment by fire, I am very convinced that Jesus never went to such place called hell as He described to the listeners. Jesus might also have used the word "Gehenna" as the Webster's New World Hebrew Dictionary defines "Hell" as "Geyheenom."[62] This "Geyheenom" sounds like "Gehenna" in

---

[60] Holman Bible Publishers, Holman Illustrated Bible Dictionary, (Nashville, 2012), p.745.
[61] Ibid.
[62] Webster's, Webster's New World Hebrew Dictionary, (China, 2010), p.606.

Greek. Just like the word "Jesus" in English is not the correct pronunciation of the Hebrew word of "Ye-shu-wah," the Hebrew word, "Geyheenom," Jesus used to describe the eternal punishment by fire was probably translated and written in Greek as "Gehenna." One thing is very clear here that the place Jesus described is not attractive, and the listeners would not want to end up there.

Moreover, one friend fluent in Hebrew language residing in the same prison POD tells me that "Sheol" and "Geyheenom" are the same words in Hebrew to describe "Hell," the eternal punishment for the unrighteous. This friend makes my belief stronger that Jesus more than likely used a Hebrew word to describe the eternal place of fire for those who reject His gospel.

I believe that I have provided more than enough describing what hell is through the mouth of Jesus. I also believe that I have made myself clear that Jesus never went to the eternal place called hellfire. However, some may argue that Apostle Peter wrote about Jesus preaching to some spirits in hell (1 Peter 3:19–20). Here I also want to dispel such false belief.

Based on the Gospel of Jesus Christ whose blood shed at the cross has redeemed all believing and trusting souls, I am willing to put my own faith in the redeemer on the line to dispel any teachings that puts Jesus in hell. I wholeheartedly agree with Dr. Gary D. Landers, who strongly dispels the theory that "Jesus went to Hell (the lake of fire) to deliver anyone."[63]

I believe that Apostle Peter was not saying that Jesus preached to the damned souls in hellfire as Jesus said when Peter wrote, "By which also he (Jesus) went and preached unto the spirits in prison; which sometime were disobedient, when once the longsuffering of God waited in the days of Noah" (1 Peter 3:19–20). Peter was among the hearers when Jesus was preaching hellfire messages. So Peter could have used the same word that Jesus used to describe the eternal hellfire if Peter intended to write such place. However, he used the

---

[63] Gary D. Landers, *The Theory of Jesus's Descent into Hell* (Texas, 2009), p.1.

WEST POINTER TO IMPRISONED PREACHER... WHY?

word "prison." This "prison" does not mean hell as Matthew Henry and Holman point out.

Matthew Henry's comments on "preaching unto the spirits in prison" are very clear. He writes, "Because they were dead and disembodied when the apostle speaks of them, therefore he purposely calls them spirits now in prison; not that they were in prison when Christ preached to them, as the vulgar Latin translation and the popish expositors pretend."[64]

When Henry spoke of "popish expositors,"[65] I sense that he was talking about preachers like Jimmy Swaggart. In Swaggart's "The Expositor's Study Bible," I find a very interesting commentary on Peter's difficult passages (1 Peter 3:19–20 and 2 Peter 2:4–5). Swaggart's exact words are quoted below:

"2 Peter 2:4 refers to a specific type of sin, which was actually the sin of fallen Angels cohabiting with women that took place before the Flood, and then after the Flood (Gen. 6:1–4), but cast them down to Hell (refers to "Tartarus," visited by Christ after His Death and on the Cross and immediately before His Resurrection). In fact, He preached "unto the spirits in prison," which refers to these fallen angels (1 Peter 3:19–20)."[66]

I just want to zoom right into Swaggart's comment about Jesus being in hell. I do not agree with him on this. While Swaggart refers to Jesus as preaching to the fallen angels in hell, Henry points to Noah as preaching, not Jesus Himself by quoting 2 Peter 2:5, "He went and preached, by his spirit striving with them, and inspiring and enabling Enoch and Noah to plead with them, and preach righteousness to them as a preacher of righteousness." I agree with Henry on Peter's passage in that Jesus was never in hell to do any sort of preaching at all.

---

[64] Matthew Henry, *Matthew Henry's Commentary on the Whole Bible* (Massachusetts, 2008), p.1951.
[65] Ibid.
[66] Jimmy Swaggart, *The Expositor's Study Bible* (Baton Rouge, 2010), p.2164.

Furthermore, Holman's KJV Study Bible points out the difficulty to discern what exactly Peter meant. The Holman's Study Bible expounds, "Christ preaching 'unto the spirits in prison' is extremely difficult to interpret."[67] Then it offers one plausible view: "The term 'spirits' refers to the souls of people who died in the great flood (Gen. 6–7). The preaching was done by the pre-incarnate Christ through Noah's preaching to disobedient contemporaries, while Noah made preparations for the flood."[68] I fully agree with the Holman's Study Bible that Jesus was not preaching in hell at all.

Finally, Holman closes by stating, "Peter could refer to Noah's contemporaries as the 'spirits in prison' because when he wrote this letter they had long been dead, were incorporeal spirits, and were under confinement awaiting God's final judgment."[69] Definitely I do not see that Peter meant hell in his epistle. Holman's view of "awaiting God's judgment" in "prison" leads me to Dr. D. R. Vestal's view on the Old Testament (OT) "Sheol" as a temporary place, not a permanent hell.[70]

The CBI course material states that Dr. Vestal offers "the opposite opinions"[71] of Dr. Landers's emphatic dispelling of Jesus ever going to hell. But I find Dr. Vestal's opinions as siding with Dr. Landers' view. I fully concur with Dr. Vestal that Jesus never went to hell, the eternal place of punishment by fire, as Jesus preached in the gospels.

Dr. Vestal concludes that "the Greek word, Gehenna, is equivalent to the Lake of Fire, and this is the place where all of the unrighteous people throughout history will be tormented forever (along with

---

[67] Holman Bible Publishers, Holman King James Version Study Bible, (Nashville, 2012), p.2090.
[68] Ibid.
[69] Ibid.
[70] Donald R. Vestal, *The Opposite Opinions of Jesus Going to Hell* (Texas, 1991), p.31.
[71] Cypress Bible Institute, "Jesus in Hell" (Garden Grove, 1991), p.2.

WEST POINTER TO IMPRISONED PREACHER… WHY?

the Devil and his Demons).”[72] He also concludes that "Gehenna" is what most people probably associate with the English word "Hell."[73] Now this permanent place does not fit with any biblical place that Jesus would have ever and never been.

I cannot picture my Lord, the Savior and the Redeemer, ever being in hell when I sing the hymn written in 1874 by Robert Lowry, "Low in the Grave He Lay:"

> Low in the grave He lay; Jesus my savior!
> Waiting the coming day; Jesus my Lord!
> Up from the grave He arose,
> With a mighty triumph O'er His foes;
> He arose a Victor from the dark domain,
> And He lives forever with His saints to reign,
> He arose! He arose!
> Hallelujah! Christ arose!

Preaching the good news of Jesus Christ to all earthly souls is to save them from burning in eternal hellfire as Jesus preached.

Before I close this paper, I want to share my conversation with Chaplain Donald Stine at Buckingham Correctional Center, where I am imprisoned. As I bid farewell to him as he retired, I asked him about the origin of Jesus descending in hell in the Apostle's Creed. He humbly replied, "Oh, I have never thought about that before. Let me get back to you." I thought he was going to just fade away on his retirement. But to my surprise, the chaplain gave me his finding as quoted below:

"I can't find the exact Greek word used in the Creed in the New Testament. It might be there, but the word simply refers to the bottom or the lower part. Old translations into English, French, and

---

[72] Vestal, p.31.
[73] Ibid.

Spanish translate the whole phrase as descended into hell. Any word for hell in the Greek, just isn't there, as I see it, except by implication."

This retiring chaplain, an ordained Baptist minister of the Gospel of Jesus Christ, is another example supporting my belief that Jesus never descended into hell.

Moreover, when I recently asked Rev. Dr. Byung H. Lee, my mentor pastor from my Sunday school days between 1975 and 1979, the same question, he reiterated my theme that Jesus did not have to go to hell. Pastor Lee shared with me Hebrews 9:27, "Just as man is destined to die once, and after that to face judgment," to point out that the people on earth have no second chance after death.

The Bible has many difficult passages to comprehend. Pastor Lee also pointed out that 1 Peter 3:19, "Through whom also he [Jesus] went and preached to the spirits in prison" is one such difficult passage in the Bible. Pastor Lee reminded me that we shall face two choices after death; eternal life or punishment. Most assuredly, I do concur with him in that Jesus's calling for us Christians is to lead as many souls as we can to avoid the eternal hellfire punishment.

Going back to my questioning Jesus's descending into the hell in the Apostles' Creed, I want to share one more relevant writing by Dr. Wayne Grudem, research professor of Bible and theology at Phoenix Seminary. He writes, "Although the phrase 'he descended into hell' does not occur in the Bible, its appearance in the widely used Apostles' Creed has generated much discussion as to its meaning and implications."[74] Dr. Grudem cites Philip Schaff's book, *The Creeds of Christendom*, to point out the murky background behind the history of the phrase "he descended into hell."[75] I just would like the following exact writing from Dr. Grudem to point out my theme of this dissertation:

---

[74] Wayne Grudem, *Bible Doctrine, Essential Teachings of the Christian Faith* (Michigan, 1999), p.257.
[75] Ibid., p.258.

WEST POINTER TO IMPRISONED PREACHER... WHY?

"Unlike the Nicene Creed and the Chalcedonian Definition, the Apostles' Creed was not written or approved by a single church council at one specific time, but rather developed gradually from about A.D. 200 to 750. A summary of the Creed's development by the great church historian Philip Schaff shows that the phrase in question was not found in any early versions of the Creed. Prior to A.D. 650, the phrase 'he descended into hell' appeared in only one version of the Creed, by Rufinus in A.D. 390. Moreover, Rufinus understood the phrase simply to mean that Christ was 'buried.' In other words, he took it to mean that Christ 'descended into the grave.' (the Greek form has hades, which can mean just 'grave,' not geenna, 'hell,' place of punishment.')"[76]

The above quotation gets me back to the old inspirational hymn, "Low in the Grave He Lay," that I shared earlier. I certainly cannot see my Lord Jesus ever being in that eternal hellfire. Dr. Grudem's final words on this topic as quoted below is exactly how I feel out this "murky" topic:

"Christ in his death on the cross completely satisfied the demands of God's righteous judgment of sin and fully bore the wrath of god against that sin; there was no need for Christ to suffer further after his death on the cross."[77]

Although there are overwhelming scholarly views supporting my theme, I think that Origen's universalism should be mentioned before I close this paper. The Lord Jesus Christ taught us to watch out for false teachers like Origen and his followers who did not believe in the eternal hellfire.

I want to share a false view of Origen's follower, a monastic monk named Evagrius Ponticus, whom Diarmaid MacCulloch calls out in his book, *Christianity, The First Three Thousand Years*. He introduces Origen's writing that in the end all will be saved and that he saw divine love even in the fire of hell, which prepared humanity

---

[76] Ibid.
[77] Ibid.

for a future ecstasy. MacCulloch quoted from *The Second Part* by Issac Niveh, who also shared the same view with Origen:

"It is not [the way of] the compassionate Maker to create rational beings in order to deliver them over mercilessly to unending affliction ... for things of which He knew even before they were fashioned."[78]

Evagrius Pontius echoed Origen's universalism by repeatedly asserting that even those suffering in hell kept those imperishable seeds of virtue. MacCulloch adds, "No wonder his Church decided that he was dangerous."[79] I also believe false teachings of Origen and his followers are dangerous. We must be watchful of such teachings.

Another danger we should consider is "popish expositors" as Matthew Henry coined. Some popish tele-evangelists preach Jesus conquering hell between His death and resurrection. Conquering hell by Jesus being in that horrible location seems out of synch with the hellfire preaching done by Christ Himself. Jesus did not have to go to hell, in my view, to conquer anything because He did all that conquering on the Cross. When Jesus proclaimed on the Cross, "It is finished!" (John 19:30) that is exactly what it means. No expositions are necessary on this completed task.

In conclusion, this paper focused on the description of hell that was proceeded through the mouth of Jesus, the Lord and the Savior. Specifically, through Jesus's lips, the hellfire gospel was preached (Mark 9:43–48). Moreover, Jesus in Matthew 25 warned of two eternal destinations where "a shepherd separates the sheep from the goats. He will put the sheep on his right and the goats on his left" (vv. 32–33). Then Jesus warned the goats on the left of "eternal punishment," but promised the sheep on the right, "the righteous to eternal life" (v. 46). Jesus did not hint any second chance in the eternal hellfire. And He had no business being in hell to save any damned souls. Therefore, I am very convinced that Jesus was never in hell.

---

[78] Diarmaid MacCulloch, Christianity: The First Three Thousand Years (New York, 2009), p.250.
[79] Ibid., p.210.

CHAPTER 9

Oh, The Sabbath Is Not Saturday!

Is the Sabbath, Saturday or Sunday? Assuming the Sabbath is the Lord's Day, did the New Testament Christians change the day to the first day of the week? In my opinion, the Sabbath is neither Saturday nor Sunday of the secular week.

The Bible Sabbath is the seventh day when God rested after spending the first six days of creation with the first day being the very beginning according to Genesis 1:1. Since the beginning and the ending of each secular day of the week are the midnight, the true biblical Sabbath which begins at the sunset cannot be either Saturday or Sunday.

Affirming that God began the creation on the first day of the seven-day week and assuming that the creation began on Sunday of the pagan calendar week, then the true Sabbath begins at the sunset on Friday and ends at the sunset on Saturday. So the Ten Commandment calls for remembering[80] and observing[81] such period and keeping it holy. From this affirmation and assumption, my answer to the first question of which day was the biblical Sabbath is neither Saturday nor Sunday of the secular calendar week.

---

[80] Exodus 20:8
[81] Deuteronomy 5:12

Moreover, I see that the New Testament Christians did not change the Sabbath (the Lord's Day) to the first day of week as the question is framed. This paper will elaborate my answers to the two theme questions above. Since the creation of mankind, there have been several confusing calendar systems or methods. For example, the Solar, the Lunar, the Jewish Sacred or Civil, the Julian, the Galilean, the Judean, and so forth are perplexing. So I have chosen the modern universal calendar system to address the questions.

Furthermore, I need to point out that the New Testament Christians did not have such universal calendar system and that they had used the Jewish sacred calendar system of counting the seven-day week as numerical days, i.e., the first day of the week and the Sabbath as the seventh day of the week starting each day at the sunset.

The meaning of the Sabbath is the seventh day of rest as first commanded to the Israelites in Exodus 16. When I assume that the New Testament Christians had followed the Exodus monthly calendar as God commanded Moses to begin counting the days and the month in Exodus 12, I clearly see that the Sabbath day does not necessarily fall on the seventh day of the Moses's calendar week. I like to explain this before sharing the opinions of other Bible scholars.

God provided the manna on the fifteenth day of the second month.[82] When we assume that the first month of the year[83] consists of thirty days, the first seventh day in the second month began at sunset on the fourth day in the second month. So when God commanded the Israelites to gather the manna starting on the fifteenth day, this day was actually the third day of the seven-day week. After six days, on the twenty-first day of the second month, God commanded the Israelites to rest.[84] This seventh day does not fall on the consecutive seventh day from the first month of Moses's calendar.

---

[82] Exodus 16:1–8
[83] Exodus 12:2
[84] Exodus 12:2

WEST POINTER TO IMPRISONED PREACHER... WHY?

When the Israelites rested on this seventh day, this day was not the seventh day from the first month[85] at all. It actually falls between the second day and the third day of the seven-day week. My point is that when God instructed Moses to call that seventh day after the six days of gathering daily manna[86], that rest day was not the seventh day of the Moses's consecutive weekly calendar. If we were to look at it from the modern secular calendar, the rest day so happens to be either Monday or Tuesday.

As a result, the modern-day Sabbath keepers (who believe the secular Saturday is the seventh day of the Exodus rest) appear to get the days confused. I do not doubt that God commanded Moses to call that seventh day "a holy Sabbath to the Lord" and "have the people rested."[87] However, I cannot find any convincing evidences in the Bible that the Genesis seventh day and the Moses's seventh day coincide on the same day. Zondervan Compact Bible Dictionary points out that "The biblical records are silent regarding the observance of the Sabbath day from creation to the time of Moses."[88]

However, one thing is very clear that God in the beginning rested on the seventh day[89] and that God has continued to work from the beginning.[90] Then God's chosen people began resting on the seventh day of the Moses's calendar[91] whose Jewish tradition has begun. This does not support that such Sabbath rest day falls on either Saturday or Sunday in the pagan secular week.

I would be amiss if I skip to mention the fourth commandment in the Ten Commandments given to the Israelites on two historic occasions in Exodus 20 and Deuteronomy 6. Exodus 20 calls them to remember the seventh day of the Moses's seven-day calendar

---

[85] Exodus 12:2
[86] Exodus 16:26
[87] Exodus 16:23–30
[88] Zondervan, *Zondervan's Compact Bible Dictionary* (Grand Rapid, 1993), p.98.
[89] Genesis 2:2
[90] John 5:17
[91] Exodus 16:23

and keep it holy. God wanted them to remember the creation in the beginning and imitate God's rest on the seventh day.[92] I want to point out here that God did not require anyone in the Genesis beginning to rest like God did.

However, many centuries after the Genesis beginning, God commanded the Israelites to begin resting on the seventh day remembering God's resting after the six days of creation. This command was based on the monthly calendar God directed Moses to keep in Exodus 16 as he led the Israelites out of their bondage in Egypt. On the other hand, Deuteronomy 6 calls them to remember God's delivering them out of Egypt as they rest on the seventh day, the Sabbath. On both accounts of the fourth commandment on the Sabbath keeping, Exodus 20 and Deuteronomy 6 are not clear whether the Genesis seventh day is the same day as the Exodus seventh day.

I agree with *Matthew Henry Commentary on the Whole Bible* that the Genesis and Exodus seventh days were probably not the same days. Henry comments on the fourth commandment in Exodus 20:8–10, "They are told what is the day they must religiously observe a seventh, after six days' labor; whether this was the seventh by computation from the first seventh, or from the day of their coming out of Egypt, or both, is not certain; now the precise day was notified to them (Ex.16:23), and from this they were to observe the seventh."[93]

Regarding the first day worship, in my view, the New Testament Christians chose the first day of the week to remember the day Jesus Christ was resurrected from the grave. They began remembering the Lord's resurrection day and the supernatural empowerment day (the Pentecost) by the coming of the Lord's Spirit where both days so happen to be the first day of the week.[94] I do strongly believe that the early followers of Jesus Christ recognized this first day of the week,

---

[92] Exodus 20:10
[93] Matthew Henry, *Matthew Henry's Commentary on the Whole Bible* (Massachusetts, 2008), p.93.
[94] John 20:1; Acts 2:1 (the day Pentecost is the fiftieth day, the first day after seven weeks)

the modern-day Sunday, to be the Sabbath. However, I do not believe that this first day was called "the Sabbath day or the Lord's Day" where such day is changed from Saturday to Sunday of the pagan week. Here I just want to share few references to support my assertion that the early Christians began recognizing the resurrection day to conduct worship services and one reference which discount my belief.

First, I want to share Holman King James Version (KJV) Study Bible which comments on Revelation 1:10 where "the Lord's day" is mentioned for the very first and the last time in the Bible. It states, "The Lord's day is likely a phrase referring to the first day of the week—Sunday, the day of resurrection—which had become the day of worship for Christians."[95] It also gives the scripture references, Acts 20:7 and 1 Corinthians 16:2.

In addition to the Holman's commentary above, Henry adds, "It was the Lord's Day, the day which Christ had separated and set apart for himself, as the Eucharist is called the Lord's Supper. Surely this can be no other than the Christian Sabbath, the first day of the week, to be observed in remembrance of the resurrection of Christ."[96]

Furthermore, I join Henry's rallying call to the followers of Christ to rejoice in the first day of the week as the Lord's Day. He ends his comment on Rev. 1:10 with "Let us who call him our Lord honor him on his own day, the day which the Lord hath made and in which we ought to rejoice."

Zondervan explains the Lord's Day as "a day especially associated with the Lord Jesus Christ, the first day of the week on which Christ arose. It was the resurrection victory on that day which marked it as distinct and sacred to the Christian Church. The Gospel emphasis upon 'the first day of the week' as the day of resurrection stresses its distinctiveness."[97]

---

[95] Holman Bible Publishers, Holman King James Version Study Bible, (Nashville, 2012), p.2131.
[96] Henry, p.1983.
[97] Zondervan, p.327.

In my belief and thought, Apostle John knew how to call a day "the Sabbath day" if it were the seventh day of the week. So I do not think he spoke these words on either the seventh day or the first day of the Jewish week. Convincingly, as he was in the Lord's "Spirit" in Rev. 1:10, I believe that John called the day "the Lord's day" not because that day was the resurrection day, the first day of the week. However, traditionally, the followers of Christ for many centuries have called the secular Sunday as "the Lord's day." They believe that John associated the resurrection day, the day after the seventh day Sabbath, with "the Lord's day."

I personally do not share the same belief because there is no proof that the day when John called "the Lord's day," was indeed either the first day or the seventh day of the week. It could have been any day of the week. Anyhow, John could have called the day, "the Sabbath," if it were the seventh day of the week or "the resurrection day" if it were the first day of the week. Since John was a Jew whose tradition of worship and rest on that Sabbath day had been ingrained in his mind during his entire life, John could have called the day what it traditionally was. As far as I am concerned, every day is the Lord's day. However, I set aside one day, the secular Sunday, for a corporate worship, and I absolutely do not mind calling that set-aside day "the Lord's day."

On the subject of the Sabbath worship and rest, Zondervan comments in a remarkable way, "The early Christians, most of whom were Jews, kept the seventh day as a Sabbath, but since the resurrection of their Lord was the most blessed day in their lives, they began very early also to meet for worship on the first day of the week (Acts 2:1), and designated it as the Lord's day. As the split between the Jews and Christians widened, the Christians came gradually to meet for worship only on the Lord's Day and gave up the observance of the seventh day."[98]

---

[98] Ibid., p.512.

William MacDonald in "The Letter to the Galatians" affirms Zondervan's observation. He states, "The one commandment which is not repeated is the one commanding Sabbath observance (in the New testament). Christians are never taught to keep the Sabbath." MacDonald goes further by emphasizing that "Christ and not the law is the believer's rule of life (1 John 2:6). He is our standard, our pattern, our example (John 13:15; 15:12; Eph. 5:1–2, 8, 15–16; 1 John 3:16)."[99]

MacDonald also suggests avoiding arguing that such Sabbath-keeping is either the ceremonial or the moral law. He ensures that "Christians are not obligated to keep the Sabbath." MacDonald gives many New Testament verses to support his claim that while the Sabbath-keeping commandment in the Ten Commandments was only for the Israelites, "the other nine commandments are repeated in the New Testament, not as law, but as instruction for those under grace."[100]

I want to share one more assertion by MacDonald before referencing an opposing view on this Sabbath keeping matter. MacDonald provides an additional note where "No gentile was ever commanded to keep the Sabbath. Although God Himself rested on the seventh day, He did not command anyone else to do it at that time. Sabbath-keeping was first commanded at Mt. Sinai, and then only to the children of Israel."[101] I am a gentile Christian, and I share the thoughts of MacDonald.

However, there are some who believe that the Sabbath-keeping commandment "was never abrogated by divine command"[102] as emphatically states in *The Lord's Day* by Colin D. Standish and Russel R. Standish. Their 359-page book goes into very details and argues that "evidence supports that the apostles continued to keep the

---
[99] William MacDonald, *The Letter to the Galatians* (Dubuque, 2011), pp.62–63.
[100] Ibid.
[101] Ibid.
[102] Colin D. Standish and Russel R. Standish, *The Lord's Day* (Rapidan, 2011), p.50. and p.60.

seventh day Sabbath holy throughout their life time."[103] Praying for God's blessing their souls of the Standish brothers and the Adventists, I want to share my opinion and the views of other theologians.

In my opinion as the first of the day week worshipper, I find the Standish brothers failing to mention that the modern secular Saturday is the biblical seventh day. I personally do not have any issue with the Sabbath-keeping worshippers who keep the modern-day Saturday as the Sabbath. Such practice assumes that the first day creation in the Genesis beginning had occurred on the modern secular Sunday. What if the Genesis creation so happens to be on the modern secular Tuesday? Then, the seventh day from the creation first day falls on the modern secular Monday. The Standish brothers does not convince me that the modern secular Saturday is indeed the seventh day from the Genesis creation day, the first day of the week.

Another point the Standish brothers make is that "It would be inconsistent and illogical for God…to have altered the seventh day Sabbath to Sunday in the Christian era when from one end of the Bible to the other…the seventh day is the only Sabbath of God provided for the blessing of His faithful people."[104] As one of God's faithful people, I see no connection here between the seventh day and the modern secular Saturday.

While the Standish brothers make a connection between the first day of the week and the modern secular Sunday, they do not associate the seventh day Sabbath with the secular Saturday. I respect those who worship on Saturday thinking Saturday is the seventh day Sabbath; however, I do not want them to impose their Saturday-keeping theology and accuse me and others who set aside the first day (secular Sunday) of the universally recognized week for corporate worship of disobeying God's commandment to keep the seventh day Sabbath holy.

---

[103] Ibid., p. 60.
[104] Ibid., p.128.

WEST POINTER TO IMPRISONED PREACHER... WHY?

As a theology student, I have not found any evidence that the Lord's day, as I have already explained my view on Revelation 1:10, is the first day of the week or the modern secular Sunday. Moreover, I am not yet convinced that the Genesis creation, the very first day of the week, began on the modern secular Sunday. As far as I am concerned, the Genesis creation could have been any one day of the seven days in the modern secular week.

I find true rest and peace in Romans 14:5–8 which the Standish brothers left out in their investigation of "a dozen references…to see whether the seventh-day Sabbath was still the valid worship day for the emerging Christian church."[105] Although they analyzed all "twelve statements in the order that they appear in the Scripture of the New Testament,"[106] they failed to analyze the statement in Romans. My deep conviction comes from Romans 14:5–6, "One man esteemeth one day above another; another esteemeth every day alike. Let every man be fully persuaded in his own mind. He that regardeth the day, regardeth it unto the Lord."

In addition to my quoting the above Scripture, I want to share the supportive assertion made by Bishop D. R. Vestal, PhD, chancellor and founder of Cypress Bible Institute. He states "Concerning Sabbath days: If the Law of Moses, including the fourth commandment[107], was in force in the New Covenant, the above statements[108] would never have been written by Paul. Each Christian can do as he pleases concerning the Sabbath and he is not to be judged by his brother 'any more.'"[109]

---

[105] Ibid., p. 52.
[106] Ibid.
[107] Exodus 20:8–11, "Remember the Sabbath day by keeping it holy" and Deuteronomy 5:12–15, "Observe the Sabbath day by keeping it holy" (NIV)
[108] My citing Romans 14:5–6 in the proceeding paragraph and D. R. Vestal's citing Romans 14:1–13, Galatians 2:3 and Galatians 5:1–5 in his writing below.
[109] Donald R. Vestal, *The Sabbath, Are Christians Obligated to Observe the 7th Day Sabbath Today?* (Cypress Bible Institute: 1991), p.3.

In my own mind, I am a persuaded man who regards every day alike unto the Lord Jesus. I happen to view all seven days in the modern secular week to be God's blessed days. I chose Sunday as a set-aside day of worship not because I believe Sunday is the Genesis Sabbath, the seventh day. Moreover, the Standish brothers in their book, *the Lord's Day*, attempt to hold me accountable to the Fourth Commandment in the Ten Commandments which commanded the Israelites to rest on the seventh day. I do not doubt that the Israelites rested in the desert on the seventh day as commanded by God in Exodus 16. They had no choice because the Sabbath-keeping was a matter of life and death. But I am not persuaded in my heart and mind that I need to follow this outdated commandment. Even if the Sabbath-keeping commandment were still valid, the pagan Saturday cannot be proven to be the Genesis seventh day. Furthermore, I agree with William MacDonald that the Sabbath-keeping, the resting on the seventh day, was only for God in the Genesis beginning.

Moreover, I find no evidence of the Sabbath keeping in the Book of Joshua either. As soon as Joshua led the Israelites into the Promised Land, the daily heavenly food ceased. The Israelites for the first time in forty years enjoyed unleavened bread and cooked grains from the new land. I believe the Sabbath rest commandment also ceased at that time; otherwise, Joshua could have emphasized the Sabbath rest and worship as soon as they entered the Promised Land.

I would like to discuss one more argument the Standish brothers and the Seventh Day Adventists make. They insist that the believers like me who do not keep Saturday as the God's mandated Sabbath are missing God's promised blessings.[110] I humbly beg to differ on this argument on two main reasons.

First, I do feel blessed by God even though I do not believe the pagan Saturday to be the Genesis seventh day. Although I do not

---

[110] Ibid., p. 233. (Isaiah 56:1–7)

participate in a corporate worship on Saturday, I thank God for the undeserving grace as promised in Genesis through the seed (Jesus) of Abraham.

Second, I strongly believe that there is no clear evidence in the Bible that the modern pagan Saturday in the secular calendar is the Genesis seventh day, the true Sabbath. Genesis 1:14 shows that God put the solar system "in the expanse of the sky (NIV)" or "in the firmament of the heaven (KJV)" on the fourth day. This means that the very first three days were not based on the solar system on which the pagan calendar is based.

Genesis 1:14 also shows that God put the solar system "to serve as signs to mark seasons and days and years." So the days after the Genesis fourth day have been based on the solar system. The Bible calendar, the Jewish sacred calendar, did not begin until God commanded Moses to begin counting the days (Exodus 12) initiating the feast of the Passover. Back then, the secular pagan calendar based on the sun and the moon was not even conceived. My point here is that neither Saturday nor Sunday of the pagan calendar based on the solar system could be the Bible Sabbath, the seventh day. Such point is unequivocally my answer to the first question of this paper, "Is the Sabbath, Saturday or Sunday?"

I would like to elaborate my answer to the second question of this theme, "Why was the Sabbath (the Lord's Day) changed by the New Testament (NT) Christians to the first day of the week?" I strongly believe that the NT Christians did not change the Sabbath (the Lord's Day) to the first day of week. Exodus 16:26 starts calling the seventh day for the first time in the Bible as "rest ... the Sabbath" and "a Sabbath unto the Lord" (Ex.16:25). Exodus 20:10 even calls the seventh day, "the Sabbath of the LORD thy God."

So the NT is very clear in that the seventh day as mandated by the High Priest had been kept according to the Old Testament, the Law. I do not argue that Jesus and his followers had kept the seventh day worship in the synagogue. They did call that day "the Sabbath." There are also evidences of the followers of Jesus meeting to honor the Lord Jesus on the first day of the week, the day after the Sabbath.[111]

While the theme question seems to equate the Sabbath with "the Lord's Day," I am uncomfortable with such equation because Revelation 1:10 is unclear whether Apostle John was using the term, "the Lord's Day," to mean the seventh day Sabbath. Likewise, the Apostle did not make it clear whether he was referring to the first day (the resurrection day) of the week either. John had known from the NT which day to call "the Sabbath day, the day after the Sabbath, or the first day of week."

I see no evidence in the Bible that the NT Christians had habitually called the Sabbath, "the Lord's day." Moreover, Apostle John did not make "the Lord's Day" clear whether he was calling the day the Sabbath or the first day of the week, I have concluded that the Sabbath cannot unequivocally be equated with "the Lord's Day." Furthermore, I do not believe John intended to change the Sabbath keeping to the first day of the week either. My personal opinion, however, leans toward "the Lord's Day" being the first day of the week. I am not talking about the secular Sunday though.

Here I am compelled to share the argument of the Adventists or other Saturday worshipers. They argue that Constantine and the Pope changed the Sabbath to Sunday from Saturday. Assuming that the first day of the early Christian era is the secular Sunday, I like to quote Dr. Vestal's writing to dispel that the NT Christians like Constantine and the Pope of that day changed the Sabbath (the seventh day) to Sunday (the first day) of the week.

Dr. Vestal cites five historic NT Christian documents to dispute such false argument, and I just want to quote just two of the five in this paper:

The Encyclopedia Britannica under "Sabbath" and "Sunday" says "In the early Christian Church Jewish Christians continued to

---

[111] John 20:19, 26; Acts 2:1 (Pentecost, the day after seven Sabbath days); Acts 20:7; and 1 Corinthians 16:2

keep the Sabbath…Paul from the first days of Gentile Christianity, laid it down definitely that the Jewish Sabbath was not binding on Christians…in 321 AD, Constantine made the Christian Sabbath, Sunday, the rest day for the Roman Empire, but it was observed by Christians for nearly 300 years before it became a law of Constantine."[112]

The New International Encyclopedia on "Sunday" says, "For some time after the foundation of the Christian Church the converts from Judaism still observed the Jewish Sabbath to a greater or lesser extent, at first, it would seem, concurrently with the celebration of the first day; but before the end of the apostolic period, Sunday, known as the Lord's day, had thoroughly established itself as the special day to be sanctified (set apart) by rest from secular labor and by public worship. The hallowing of the fourth century; and the Emperor Constantine confirmed the custom by a law of the state."[113]

Moreover, I do unhesitatingly believe that the NT Christians began meeting on the first day of the week to honor the Lord Jesus. I am not suggesting that they changed the Sabbath keeping to the first day of the week from the seventh day of the week.

Jesus never ordered such change either, but He said, "Son of man (Jesus Himself) is Lord also of the Sabbath."[114] So I want to follow Jesus's saying in John 5:17, "My Father worketh hitherto, and I work" (KJV) or "My Father is always at his work to this very day, and I, too, am working" (NIV). Jesus was not calling for a change in the Sabbath keeping on the first day of the week, but I believe that Jesus was saying in my own words, "Work like me every day for the Creator God has never stopped working."

The Sabbath keepers on the secular Saturday thinking this day is the Genesis seventh day may disagree with me by quoting the Exodus Sabbath commandment that mandated the Israelites to rest on the

---

[112] Vestal. P.16.
[113] Ibid.
[114] Matthew 12:8; Mark 3:28

seventh day. However, I go back to Jesus by paraphrasing His words, "Do not worry about the days, but honor the Lord continually, each and every day."[115] Jesus's words about putting the worry aside about the days are echoed by Apostle Paul in Colossians 2:16 and Romans 14:5–6. I also believe Joshua set the tone for Jesus in Joshua 24:15, "Choose you this day whom ye will serve ... but as for me and my house we will serve the Lord." I choose every day to honor my Lord Jesus, and I choose to set aside the first day of the secular week to honor my Lord's resurrection and His Spirit's miraculous filling and empowerment on the Pentecost.

There are many evidences of the early Christians Christianizing pagan worship days. One example is Christianizing Sunday, the day for the sun worship during the Roman Empire. As mentioned in Chapter 7, "Who Is The Father of the Baby?" The Bible has already declared Jesus as "the Sun of righteousness" (Mal. 4:2) and "the rising Sun" (Luke 1:78).

Consequently, Sunday, in my view, has already Christianized to worship Jesus. That day is Jesus's day. So, I echo the calling of Joshua again, "Choose you this day whom ye will serve..." Our Creator seems to be saying to us, "You decide which day you want to sabbath-rest and worship me corporately!"

I do strongly believe the true Sabbath, the true rest, is in the Lord Jesus. If we love the Lord Jesus with all our hearts, the Sabbath should reside in our hearts. We are to serve our Lord Jesus and no other gods. The days themselves could become gods, and we need to be careful as not to worship the days and lose focus our spiritual eyes and ears to our Lord who is above all including the days.

In summary, I do not believe that either Saturday or Sunday in the secular pagan calendar week is the Sabbath, the Genesis seventh day of the God's week. There is no evidence in the entire Bible to pinpoint one day of the pagan week to be the Genesis first day of God's week. Also, I do not believe that New Testament Christians changed

---

[115] Matthew 12:1–13; Mark 2:23–28; Luke 6:1–11

the Sabbath (the Lord's Day) to the first day of the week either. I do believe that they chose the Lord's resurrection day and the Pentecost (Acts 2) which were the first day of the week to honor Jesus.

The Bible is very clear that God's creation commenced in the beginning on the first day out of the seven-day week. We do not know for sure on which day of the secular week the Genesis first day falls. During the human history, there have been several calendar systems such as the Solar, the Lunar, the Julian, the Galilean, the Judean, and so forth. Instead of arguing about which day is the Sabbath or "the Lord's Day." We should be "offering our bodies as living sacrifices holy and pleasing unto the Lord"[116] every day. We should not conform to the patterns of the worldly calendars, but we should Christianize pagan days to holy and pleasing to the Lord. We should just set aside a day to assemble together as a corporate body whose head is Christ to worship and honor our Lord. So help us all, God! Amen!

---

[116] Romans 12:1

CHAPTER 10

Oh, Tithing Should Be Voluntary!

Was tithing only practiced under the Law? Absolutely, yes!

"In tithes and offerings. You are under a curse…because you are robbing me. Bring the whole tithe into the storehouse…Test me in this, and see if I will not throw open the floodgates of heaven and pour out so much blessing hat you will not have room enough for it." (Malachi 3:9–10, NIV)

"Give to Caesar what is Caesar's, and to God what is God's." (Luke 20:25, NIV)

"Set aside a sum of money in keeping with his income." (1 Corinthians 16:2, NIV)

"God loves a cheerful giver." (2 Corinthians 9:7, NIV)

Tithing or giving God the very first 10 percent of income is one of theologically debated subjects. Was tithing only practiced under the Law in the Old Testament (OT) era? Does tithing still apply today under the grace in the New Testament (NT) era? My answer is absolute yes to the former and caveat yes to the latter. This paper will attempt to explain my answers, and I need to state the caveat now before proceeding. There is no evidence of any teachings by either Lord Jesus or His disciples in the NT mandating the Christians to give the tithe to the church.

My research and experience have shown that only the Christian minority do tithe. While some may tithe because they feel obligated under the Law, some may do it from their own personal understanding and belief of the biblical teaching on tithing. In my view, the Christians should tithe more than just money; i.e., time (2.4 hour/day or 144 minutes/day). Actually, we the Christians, should give more than just the tithe (10 percent) of our resources (money, time, dedication, etc.) for advancing the gospel of Jesus Christ to expand His Kingdom.

First, I want to share how the Barna Group, Ltd., defines "Origins of Tithing" as a frame of reference for this paper. I will just quote below the exact words from the Barna's published research paper, and then I will follow up with its shocking research finding on the tithing trend since 2000 in the discussion.

"Strangely, tithing is a Jewish practice, not a Christian principle espoused in the New Testament. The idea of a tithe—which literally means one-tenth or the tenth part—originated as the tax that Israelites paid from the produce of the land to support the priestly tribe (the Levites), to fund Jewish religious festivals, and to help the poor. The ministry of Jesus Christ, however, brought an end to adherence to many of the ceremonial codes that were fundamental to the Jewish faith. Tithing was just a casualty. Since the first-century, Christians have believed in generous giving, but have not been under any obligation to contribute a specific percentage of their income."[117]

Yes, tithing was only practiced under the OT Law by defining "practiced" as obeyed by the Israelites, God's chosen people, as ordered by God through Moses in that era. However, Christians in the NT era under the grace, meaning no longer under the Mosaic

---

[117] New Study Shows Trends in Tithing and Donating, Barna Group, Limited (www.barna.group), 2011

Law, should practice more than just tithing of personal income. In my humble view, any giving or offering to God should be done cheerfully and voluntarily without anything (i.e., the Law) or anyone (i.e., clergyman) obligating them to do so.

Certainly, Christians are not ordered to tithe in the NT. Such practice today is not a life and death matter like the OT days; thus, the Barna finds only a small percentage of Christians do tithe to support their local churches. This finding may surprise the reader. It's fitting here that I share the interesting result of the Barna in the following before I proceed:

"The percentage of adults who tithe has stayed constant since the turn of the decade, falling in the 5% to 7% range. The Barna tracking reported that the proportion of adults who tithe was 7% in 2006 and 2005; 5% in 2004 and 2003; 6% in 2002; and 5% in 2001."[118]

The tithers today may have various reasons for tithing; however, in my strong view, the Lord Jesus has never commanded anyone to tithe. Neither did the Apostles mention such tithing. I find Apostle Paul asking the Galatians and the Corinthians to make offerings without mentioning the word "tithe" and to give according to their abilities to give.

In 1 Corinthians 16:2, we can observe that Apostle Paul reached out to each Galatian and each Corinthian to "set aside a sum of money in keeping with his income" (NIV) or "lay by him in store, as God hath prospered him" (KJV). Holman KJV Bible Study comments that each one was asked to make offerings "based on his ability to give."[119] This tells me that the Galatians and the Corinthians were not ordered like the Israelites under the law.

---

[118] Ibid.
[119] Holman Bible Publishers, Holman King James Version Study Bible, (Nashville, 2012), p.1930.

WEST POINTER TO IMPRISONED PREACHER... WHY?

Based on the words of Jesus Christ, "It is more blessed to give than receive"[120] and the teaching of Paul, "God loveth a cheerful giver,"[121] the Galatians and the Corinthians probably gave cheerfully without any law or order brought upon them. However, some may argue that the tithing under the law still apply today.

First, I should define what is meant by "under the law" before proceeding to address the application of tithing today under the grace. "Under the law" in this paper is defined as the Israelites practicing the Mosaic Law under which tithing falls. I mention the Mosaic Law because I agree with Zondervan Compact Bible Dictionary that tithing's "origin is unknown, but it goes back far beyond the time of Moses."[122]

Beyond the time of Moses, the dictionary mentions Abraham and Jacob tithing. It shows Abraham's giving "tithes to Melchizedek"[123] and Jacob's promising tithes to God[124] Abraham and Jacob were not yet "under the law." However, Zondervan notes, "Mosaic law required tithing of all produce of land and herds (Leviticus 27:30–33); used for support of Levites and priests (Numbers 18:21–32); additional tithes may have been required at certain times (Deuteronomy 12:5–18; 14:22–29); there were penalties for cheating in tithing (Leviticus 27:31; Deut. 26:13–15)."[125]

Even during the New Testament period, Zondervan comments that "Pharisees tithed even herbs (Matthew 22:23; Luke 11:42)."[126] However, I find Jesus only used the word "tithe" twice; once in a parable to point out a Pharisee praying to show off his tithing while comparing himself to others and the other in a rebuke to hypocritical

---

[120] Acts 20:35
[121] 2 Corinthians 9:7
[122] Zondervan, Zondervan's Compact Bible Dictionary, (Grand Rapid, 1993), p.587.
[123] Genesis 14:20; Hebrews 7:2, 6.
[124] Genesis 28:22.
[125] Zondervan, p.588.
[126] Ibid.

religious leaders like the Pharisee who practiced external religious rituals like tithing instead of internal virtues such as "justice, mercy and faithfulness."

Jesus's parable and the rebuke do not discourage tithing, but he is more focused on the internal goodness. What I like to point out is that Jesus never reminded the hearers of the tithing under the Mosaic Law that must be practiced. Jesus also taught the hearty giving as opposed to showy giving. In my strong opinion, any giving including tithing to the church has to come from the heart, not by any law or church mandates.

However, the early church under the leadership of the Pope might have mandated the tithing to the church. Diarmaid MacCulloch wrote in his book, *Christianity: The First Three Thousand Years Christianity*, about such tithing mandate where he said, "Other great financial change in the church's medieval past, the financing of parish priests by tithes."[127] MacCulloch's account is worth a quote as below:

"As parishes were organized, it became apparent that there were now sources of wealth for churchmen as well as for secular landlords. The parish system covering the countryside gave the Church the chance to tax the new farming resources of Europe by demanding from its farmer-parishioners a scriptural tenth of agricultural produce, the tithe. Tithe was provided by many more of the laity than the old aristocratic elite, and was another incentive for extending the Church's pastoral concern much more widely."[128]

MacCulloch's account is why I answered yes to the question in the introduction, "Does tithing still apply today under the grace?" During my spiritual growth of more than forty years, I have attended many churches as I had moved around several times as a soldier in the US Army. Although I have not seen any written church mandate of tithing to church members, I had sensed an unwritten mandate

---

[127] Diarmaid MacCulloch, *Christianity: The First Three Thousand Years* (New York, 2009), p.932.
[128] Ibid. p. 369.

WEST POINTER TO IMPRISONED PREACHER... WHY?

where the church leadership positions required tithing. I find such requirement unbiblical in that the apostles never required tithing as any requirements to become a church leader.

Tithing was only a requirement, a practice, mandated under the Mosaic Law to the Israelites. I want share how Holman Illustrated Bible Dictionary defines tithe and conclude this paper by sharing my final thoughts on this tithing matter.

Holman echoes Zondervan's definition of tithing as mandated under the Mosaic Law. In addition, Holman shows, "The Deuteronomic code stipulated that the tithe of agricultural produce be used for a family feast at the sanctuary celebrating God's provision (Deuteronomy 14:22–27). The same code stipulated third year's tithe for care of the Levites, orphans, widows, and foreigners (Deuteronomy 14:28–29). Some scholars think the differences in legislation reflect different uses of the tithe at various stages of Israel's history."[129]

Holman also talks about the NT period where "the Rabbis understood the laws as referring to three separate tithes: a Levitical tithe, a tithe spent celebrating in Jerusalem, and a charity tithe."[130] It also mentions Malachi 3:8 where neglecting the tithe is equated with robbing God. This robbing God scripture was used by church leaders to imply that tithing was a practice mandate from God even under the grace. I personally have hard time accepting such rationale.

My final thoughts go back to the words of the Lord Jesus in Luke 11:42, "Woe to you Pharisees, because you give God a tenth of your mint, rue and all other kinds of garden herbs, but you neglect justice and the love of God. You should have practiced the latter without leaving the former undone." I do agree with Matthew Henry's commentary in this verse where Jesus rebuked the Pharisees "for laying

---

[129] Holman Bible Publishers, Holman Illustrated Bible Dictionary, (Nashville, 2012), pp. 1600–1601.
[130] Ibid.

stress upon trifles, and neglecting the weighty matters of the law."[131] In my strong opinion, Jesus still does not want the church leaders to lay stress on the church members by quoting Malachi 3:8 to corner the non-tithing as robbing God.

Henry's commentary on this particular reprove leads to me to my final thoughts; that is, "Now Christ does not condemn them for being so exact in paying tithes, but to think that this would atone for the neglect of their greater duties; for those laws which relate to the essentials of religion they made nothing of: You pass over judgment and the love of God, you make no conscience of giving men their dues and God your hearts." [132]

In conclusion, I strongly believe that tithing was indeed practiced under the Mosaic Law. Moreover, I do believe that tithing is still practiced under the grace with a caveat in that modern-day tithing is not a practice mandated by the Law of Moses. Just like Solomon said, "Money is the answer to everything."[133] The Church of God cannot carry out the Great Commission to preach the Gospel of Jesus Christ by serving the needy without money. However, any giving to include tithing must be done cheerfully without any mandate from any laws or clergymen.

Tithing should be taught as a voluntary and godly giving to the church, not a mandated giving regardless of differences whether under the Law or the grace. I hope and pray that the Barna Research Group soon finds a much higher percentage of Christians tithing from their hearts without any pressures from the church leadership or its biased teaching on tithing. In my strong mind and spirit, all giving of blessed resources including "the whole tithe"[134] of personal income should be done cheerfully for the preaching of the Gospel, expansion of God's Kingdom, and edification of the Church of God. Amen!

---

[131] Matthew Henry, *Matthew Henry's Commentary on the Whole Bible* (Massachusetts, 2008), p.1485.
[132] Ibid.
[133] Ecclesiastes 10:19.
[134] Malachi 3:8.

CHAPTER 11

How Could They Do That?

"Suffering is an ineradicable part of life, even as fate and death. Without suffering and death human life cannot be complete."

(Dr. Viktor Frankle, a Holocaust survivor, author of *Man's Search for Meaning*)

"God intentionally allows you to go through painful experiences to equip you for ministry to others."

(Pastor Rick Warren, the world's best-selling author of *The Purpose Driven Life*)

"Gird up thy loins like a man" (KJV) *"Brace yourself like a man"* (NIV)

(Job 38:3; 40:11)

In this chapter, the author wants to inform the reader of egregious violations of the basic human rights so that the reader can prevent oneself from experiencing the similar inhumane treatments. Ken's inhuman experiences in the interrogation room, the jail booking office, and the suicide watch chained to the hospital bed and the solitarily confined bed should be very startling to the reader.

Before we begin, Dr. Anita L. Boss needs to be introduced. Here are her credentials: Psychology Doctor (Psy.D.), American Board of Professional Psychologists (ABPP), Board Certified in Forensic Psychology.

Dr. Anita Boss: What did you mean by the devil getting into your eyes?
Ken, the Joe: Excuse me? Say it again please?
Dr. Boss: You said to the detective, "The devil has gotten into my eyes!"
Ken: What detective? I do not remember saying that to anyone.
Dr. Boss: I have the tape here in my laptop. Do you want to hear it?
Ken: Sure!
Dr. Boss: The tape is three hours long, and I need to find the place…
Ken: What? Three hours long?
Dr. Boss: Yes, you don't remember?
Ken: Wait a minute…I do remember talking to two guys for…maybe…one or two minutes. Not for three hours.

Here, keeping in line with the I[3] purpose of the book to Inform, Illuminate, and Inspire, the reader should be informed of Dr. Boss's credentials and of certain legal terms relating to interrogation. Then the reader should appreciate this chapter better. So the clear definition of legal terms such as "Interrogation, Miranda Rule, Under Influence, and Coercion" should be understood before proceeding.

Deluxe Black's Law Dictionary (sixth edition) defines:

Interrogation - In the criminal law, the process of questions propounded by police to person arrested or suspected to seek solution of crime. Such person is entitled to be informed of his rights, including right to have counsel present, and the consequences of his answers.

WEST POINTER TO IMPRISONED PREACHER... WHY?

If the police fail or neglect to give these warnings, the questions and answers are not admissible in evidence at the trial or hearing of the arrested person.

Miranda Rule - Prior to any custodial interrogation (that is, questioning initiated by law enforcement officers after a person is taken into custody or otherwise deprives of his freedom in any significant way) the person must be warned:

1. That he has a right to remain silent;
2. That any statement he does make may be used as evidence against him;
3. That he has a right to the presence of an attorney;
4. That if he cannot afford an attorney, one will be appointed for him prior to any questioning if so he desires.

Unless and until these warnings or a waiver of these rights are demonstrated at the trial, no evidence obtained in the interrogation may be used against the accused.

Note: Ken is very familiar with the Miranda Rule. He had commanded a platoon and a battery where he had used the Miranda Rule during the US Army's Uniform Code of Military Justice (UCMJ) Article 15 (disciplinary code) proceedings. Let us proceed with defining legal terms.

Mind - In the legal sense, "mind" means only the ability to will, to direct, to permit, or to assent.

In this legal sense, Ken was not in the right frame of mind to be questioned during the three-hour long interrogation which he still does not remember entirely.

Coercion - coercion that vitiates confession can be mental as well as physical, and question is whether accused was deprived of his free choice to admit, deny, or refuse to answer.

In Ken's right state of mind today, he was coerced during the unwilled interrogation. The reader is reminded here that the atrocity committed by Ken is inexcusable, but Ken did not swear and serve in the military for thirty years to defend such violation of the Miranda Rule. Let us pick up from where we left you off during Dr. Boss's evaluation interview with Ken.

Dr. Boss: Do you remember calling your wife Hannah, Happy?
Ken: No!
Dr. Boss: Then who is Happy?
Ken: Happy is the name of my dog, a poodle.

The audiotape plays groggy Ken repeating himself with "Happy" when asked few times what his wife's name was. When Ken married Hyon-Chong, he named her Hannah from the biblical story. 1 Samuel 1:9–18 tells a story of infertile Hannah, who prayed to God for a son. Hearing Hannah's prayer, God blessed her with a son, Prophet Samuel. Although Ken and Hannah had attempted to conceive for ten years, the baby did not come. So they adopted an eight-month-old girl from Korea. Ken named the baby girl, Joy.

Dr. Boss: How could they do that? Can they do that?
[Dr. Boss was referring to the unprofessional questioning by the detectives for three hours plus when Ken was out of his right mind. He was certainly incoherent as the audiotape showed.]
Ken: [His medicated alert mind went back to the hazy moment when he was confronted with two men. He remembered being so sleepy.] Wow, that's very interesting. I want to hear the whole thing.

WEST POINTER TO IMPRISONED PREACHER... WHY?

Dr. Boss: We don't have time to listen to the whole thing now. You can arrange that with your lawyer. But do you recall waiving your Miranda rights?

Ken: No! What happened?

Dr. Boss: Here, you were asked to sign the waiver documents in the beginning. But later in the tape, you asked, "Is this when my Miranda rights come in?" Then the detective replied, "You had already waived the rights. Remember?" Then there was silence.

Ken: Wow! All I remember is falling asleep. These guys did not have the video tape of me dozing off?

Dr. Boss: No. There is only the audiotape.

Ken: Wow! [Realizing that the detectives had taken advantage of Ken's groggy and sleepy condition, Ken was sickened to his stomach.]

Dr. Boss: How could they do that? [She seemed very perplexed and empathetic to the unfair questioning by the detectives. After learning that Ken was questioned against his will, Dr. Boss could not believe the crooked tactic employed by the detectives.]

Ken: Wow! [Ken knew immediately that the detectives had taken advantage of his groggy and sleepy condition still under the influence of thirteen to fifteen prescription Ambien pills he had ingested the night before. When Ken realized that only audio recording was available, he naively thought that was the normal practice. However, the court proceedings had revealed that the video recording capability was available just twenty minutes away from Fort Belvoir Criminal Investigative Division office whose recorder malfunctioned and could only record audibly. Not having groggy and sleepy Ken recorded in a video tape was advantageous to the prosecution's case. The video recording could have been a blow to the investigative work. A reasonable human being in right mind would recognize that something went wrong in Ken's interrogation where undue influence was applied. Now let us see how Black's Law Dictionary defines it.]

Undue Influence - Any improper or wrongful constraint, machination, or urgency of persuasion whereby the will of a person is overpowered and he is induced to do or forbear an act which he would not do or would do if left to act freely. Influence which deprives person influenced of free agency or destroys freedom of his will and renders it more the will of another than his own. Misuse of position of confidence or taking advantage of a person's weakness, infirmity, or distress to change improperly that person's actions or decisions.

Term refers to conduct by which a person, through his power over mind of testator, makes the latter's desires conform to his own, thereby overmastering the violation of the testator.

[Reiterating the fact that his book is not a jurisprudence document, the author desires all legal definitions laid out in this chapter convince the reader that Ken did not voluntarily permit the interrogation to continue. Regardless, Ken's being under "undue influence" should not be debatable.]

Dr. Boss: We do not have time to hear the entire three-hour long tape today, but you should arrange with your lawyer to see and hear the entire transcript of the interrogation.

Ken: Okay...thank you!

[Now, let us talk about the phrase, "Innocent until proven guilty," which requires no legal definition. Simply no person suspected of wrong doings should be treated like a criminal. Inhumane treatments should not occur in the jail or prison cells. However, when Ken was booked into the Fairfax County Adult Detention Center, horrific inhumane treatments were experienced, and this chapter will conclude with this experience.]

We are now at the booking station of the Fairfax jail on June 14, 2010.

Detective: He is suicidal.

WEST POINTER TO IMPRISONED PREACHER... WHY?

Booking officer: All right! Here you are [on top of the booking document is handwritten "Suicidal." During the court proceeding, the prosecutor convinced the judge that the jury should not see the word "Suicidal," so the word was deleted out from the document, and from that point on, the jury was led to believe that Ken was sane not only at the time of booking, but also throughout the horrendous day on June 13, 2010. Being suicidal is one of many symptoms of the clinically depressed as Ken was throughout the ordeal. Anyhow, the reader should be alarmed at what transpired as Ken was being booked and ended up at Inova Fairfax Hospital under the 24/7 suicide watch.]

Booking Officer: Need you to strip down! [He motions three other deputy guards to take care of the situation.]

Ken: [Strips down to his underwear brief. Hesitating to take the last piece off in front of overpowering guards.]

Booking Officer: The shorts too!

Ken: [Turning around as not to expose his frontal genitalia in front of the guards, Ken took his brief off as one guard with rubber gloves grabbed it. This was the worst humiliating moment in Ken's life. He kept naively thinking such was the normal intake procedure.]

Booking Officer: Now the glasses!

Ken: [just begging without arguing] I need the glasses to see and read please.

Guard#1: You won't be doing any reading. [silent chuckles by the guards.]

Guard#2: Here. [Opened the metal door of a cell. The door had an opening about 3"×18". The dimly lit cell had no bed, no chair, no window, no toilet, no sink.]

Guard #2: Here. [Ken was handed a black armless garment, a safety smock, to cover the upper body from the neck to the waist.]

Ken: [Not saying anything, Ken grabbed the smock and covered his naked upper body immediately because the cold temperature in the dungeon was unbearable. A putrid smell hit the nostril instantly.

Obviously, the stink of feces on the floor was unsanitized. A grated burrow along one side of the wall flushed as a guard pushed a button in the hallway. Ken realized that he had just walked into a torture chamber. He still calls it a nasty "dungeon," and he knew that something was not quite right. The warmth of Ken's feet turned into icy cold from the freezing floor. Something bad was about to happen.]

Guard#2: [Slammed the door shut.]

Ken: [He naively thought that what he had just experienced was the norm during the jail intake. However, this dungeon so-called Special Housing Unit for the mentally unstable was quite different from the normal Solitary Confinement, known as the Hole.]

Female Guard: Do you want some water? [She might have been the guard on duty to watch Ken. Every fifteen minutes as it seems, she had been annoyingly coming by asking the same question.]

Ken: No, thanks! [Ken was shivering badly. The dark presence or the evil spirit was getting on his nerve, his already unstable mind. He had an unfinished job. The darkness kept reminding Ken that he ought to finish it off. His body began to tremble uncontrollably. The place was putrid and so dim. Certainly, without his prescription spectacles, he was seeing a figure in the corner staring at Ken. Something bad was about to happen then.]

Female Guard: Do you want some water? [Fifteen-minute checks seemed to come so fast.]

Ken: [Shivering with his naked butt on the cold nasty floor, Ken asked himself, "Is this really happening?" The darkened figure in one corner in his blurred vision and mind called out, "You are a coward. You can't finish the job, can you? Or you will, won't you?" Then, the horrible thing did happen. A desperate self-willed or inflicted bruises would find Ken in a pool of his own blood. He still had breath.]

The author must interject here and introduce another self-willed or inflicted bruises which led to the ultimate death on the Cross at the Calvary. On the Calvary two thousand years ago, an innocent man, who claimed to be the Messiah, the Christ, or the Savior for the entire world, had inhumanely hung on a Roman execution stake for six long hours. This man was Jesus.

Referencing the words of Prophet Isaiah (52:13–53:12) and the four gospels in the New Testament, the author will let the words used by the King James Version, the New International Version, and mine to speak for themselves of the inhumane treatments Jesus had endured.

This innocent Jesus was betrayed and denied by His own disciples. Then he was mocked, beaten, blindfolded, insulted, falsely accused, ridiculed, sneered, punished, flogged, scourged, nailed, pierced, crucified, slaughtered, murdered, executed, thirsted, choked, neglected, ignored, smitten, struck, conspired, despised, marred, deformed, whipped, disfigured, and so forth.

Prophet Isaiah declared, "Yet, it pleased the Lord to bruise ... the pleasure of the LORD shall prosper in his hand" (KJV) or "Yet, it was the Lord's will to crush him and cause him to suffer, and though the Lord makes his life a guilt offering" (NIV).

How crazy or insane! How could anyone be pleased to see such torture? Who would have such will to see his beloved tormented? What father with a sane mind would be pleased to see his own child die of slow and painful suffocation? How could such inhumane method of execution be a will of a sound mind?

Only one person who ever walked on earth fits the description of the man Prophet Isaiah calls in Isaiah 53:10. That person is Jesus. Here is a paraphrased version of Isaiah's prophesy seven hundred years plus before Jesus was even born:

"Creator Yahweh wanted to crush or bruise his choice lamb, Ye-shu-a, and cause him to suffer. Then Yahweh made Ye-shu-a a guilt offering for sin. And Yahweh was pleased to see the striped, nailed, pierced, and bloodied sacrificial lamb suffocate to death."

Was the willed or pleased insane or what? Could that person be a half crazy or half insane? Such horrible unimaginable death willed by the Creator and volunteered by Jesus is theologically called the "sacrificial" and "vicarious" death. Someone without blemish or sin had to die and bleed as a sacrificial lamb to atone for the sins of the humanity. Only Jesus qualifies for that unblemished lamb. Moreover, we deserve to die, but Jesus died in our place. Why? Whether anyone likes it or not, that is the plan of ultimate atonement for the fallen humanity.

"Hey! We are going to send ya back to Jay-eel!" unprofessionally yelled the nurse on duty at the emergency room to where Ken's bloodied naked body was ambulanced.

Ken came to as the female nurse's outcry was heard repeatedly. He found himself chained to the bed; his left wrist and right ankle were cuffed with the metal restraints. These metal pieces are regulated to be inhuman where they are regulated for a temporary measure. The humane restraints consist of leather or poly.

"We are gonna send ya back to da Jay-eel!" the extremely ignorant nurse blurted out again.

Ken could not make out her face because his prescription bifocals were at the intake station. He just wanted to yell back, "Will ya just shut up!" He just could not believe that demonic nurse might be the one who inserted the catheter into Ken's penis. He also learned that a vinyl pouch laid right next to the bed.

Then one major network TV station was reporting about Ken's arrest. Of course, the reporter had to mention that he was a West Point graduate. Ken heard enough to figure out that the atrocious double-murder story was broadcasted throughout the USA.

"Yee! You gonna go right back to the Jay-eel!" the nurse just did not want to let go of her stupidity.

Ken also noticed that there were two deputy guards giggling next to the bed. Their giggling had to do with this nurse losing herself to a helpless oriental man whose bloody head is wrapped up

WEST POINTER TO IMPRISONED PREACHER... WHY?

with a neck brace holding his neck steady. Nobody in the emergency room figured out that he needed his glasses. Without them, he was somewhat blind.

Ken's inhumane treatments at the intake station and another humiliating situation with the judgmental nurse might be isolated incidents. The author does wish to emphasize that there are many professional folks serving the communities as first responders such as police and emergency medical technicians.

By the way, Ken took care of the medical bill over $70K which included the nursing service. The last things he needed was the unprofessional and condemning outcries from this particular impolite and unconscionable nurse. Other nurses who had tended to Ken's needs were professional.

The same is true with the deputy guards. The author wants to make sure the reader does not misunderstand the important message this chapter intends to deliver.

When Ken's head wounds were staple-stitched up, he was transferred to another waiting room to determine the extent of the neck injury. The X-ray and other medical scan procedures had revealed that the neck bone was cracked, requiring a surgery.

Ken had to wait few weeks for the surgery and the recovery under two deputy guards watching him 24/7. They had employed two-point metal restraints where one hand and the opposite ankle were chained to the bed 24/7. Once again, the leather and poly are humane methods of restraints. But Ken was under excessive and inhumane metal restraints. In other words, he was treated like an animal or hardened criminal.

Complying the two-point restraint and two-on-one watch instructions, the guards ran two shifts. Although unclear, the guards kept a logbook which should have indicated the time when the hand and the ankle were alternatively restrained with the metal pieces in so many hours. Ken never complained because he naively thought that was the normal method. But he realized that excessive restraints and guards were used.

Then there was no personal hygiene: no shower, no brushing teeth, no shaving. Some nurses would take the initiatives to hand Ken a wet towel, and he used one free hand to wash his face. Then there were other nurses who treated him like a hardened criminal. Then there was an annoying TV that the guards enjoyed watching. The loud TV volume along with their loud conversations drove Ken even more frustrating. It was a living hell.

The author feels it is time to conclude this chapter because the point is clearly made in that Ken had been treated inhumanly like an insane hardened criminal. Although he never demonstrated any resistance, excessive measures were used to restrain him. Basic human rights were violated.

During the month-long hospital stay to get his deep head scars stitched up (twenty-four staple ones) and his fractured neck bone bolted up (two small surgical bolts), Ken had authorized no visits except the medical and the legal staff. The author needs to mention one compassionate lawyer, a public defender, since Ken had not hired a lawyer then.

Ms. Dawn Butorac treated Ken like a normal human being. When he did not want any of his family members contacted for help, she shared her wisdom which still touches Ken's heart. When he told her that he did not want to hurt his family members, especially the youngest brother living in Virginia, Ms. Butorac responded, "Your brother would be hurt even more if he learns that you have not asked him for help." Ken needed no further wisdom. He finally authorized her to contact his brother who has endured difficulties to this day. However, Ken refused to have anyone, especially his family members, see himself chained to the hospital bed like an animal with the self-inflicted injuries to the head and the neck.

When Ken was transferred to the solitarily confined jail cell, the two-point restraint had continued. However, the guards watch was reduced to one-on-one watch 24/7. Still Ken had to suffer the metal restrains where his hand and the opposite ankle had to be chained to the bed. Once again, the metal pieces are considered inhumane when used excessively and for the extended periods. These metal pieces restricted the freedom of movements. Ken had neither showered nor shaven for six weeks. Involuntarily, he was sporting a long beard and a mustache. His repeated pleas for the confiscated bi-focal glasses were denied, and only those who need glasses to pursue happiness or comfort could understand this situation to be inhumane.

Eventually, after a few months the jail authority had to release Ken to the general population area because he had never demonstrated detrimental behaviors warranting any type of restraints. He had patiently accepted the authority's "safety reason" for not giving back the glasses. To them, the pair of glasses could have been used as an instrument to harm both the guards and Ken himself. Furthermore, the prosecution was building a case to show that Ken was sane before, during, and after the failed familicide attempt.

The verdict came down to forty years for the double murder conviction when one murder conviction could end up being the multiple life sentence without parole. Ken overheard one prisoner complaining, "I ain't kill nobody, but I am doing forty years!" For Ken's case, the prosecutor convinced the jury to believe that Ken was not crazy or insane enough even though he had been treated like an insane animal for few months.

Enduring such inhumane treatments, Ken had so many "Why?" questions like Job had in the book of Job. As soon as he was untethered from the bed, he asked for a Bible. Still under one-to-one watch 24/7, he went through the whole Bible searching for the answers.

The answers to Job's many questions did not come until the last chapters in the long book of Job. God had to call out Job twice to man up. God was also telling Ken to man up. Today is no different. Job 38:3 and 40:7, "Brace yourself like a man" (NIV) and "Gird up thy loins like a man" (KJV), need no expositions. They are exactly what they mean.

Ken had learned a huge divine lesson during the horrible inhumane conditions that his Creator was still in charge of Ken's affairs. The answer to the title of this book, *West Pointer to Imprisoned Preacher ... Why?* is for Ken to experience the sovereignty, the providence, and the provision on which he must trust and rely. The "Why?" question was clearly answered to Ken for him to "Brace" himself up like a man or "Gird up" his loins like a man and heed to the divine calling.

So many other questions did not need to be answered. Ken is pleased with the answer to the ultimate "Why?" question. Now he is an apologist for the provision of God, who is Jesus. The only provision that the Creator has given to the redemption of the fallen humanity is Jesus. Why Jesus? The purpose of this book is to illuminate the good news, the Gospel of Jesus Christ. So if the reader can bear with the author for a brief moment, hopefully Ken's hard-learned lesson and surrender to his Creator's calling to preach the Gospel should become more illuminated.

John the Baptist in John 1:29 and 36 calls Jesus "the Lamb of God." Why the Lamb? Prophet Isaiah, about seven hundred years prior to the birth of the Lamb Jesus, foretold of the one sacrificial lamb in Isaiah 53:7–8. Only human fits the description of this sacrificial lamb was Jesus. The early disciples of Jesus also called Jesus God's sacrificial lamb.

Apostle Peter wrote about Jesus in 1 Peter 1:19, "The precious blood of Christ, a lamb without blemish or defect." This lamb, God's only provision as John the Baptist calls, "takes away the sins of the world." Whether anyone believes in this divine provision or not, that is what the Bible says. And so Ken believes.

Apostle Paul said in Ephesians 1:7 (NIV), "In him [Jesus] we have redemption through his blood, the forgiveness of sins, in accordance with the riches of God's grace." This verse simply means that the payment for redeeming the fallen man is the blood of Jesus Christ, and such divine redemption is called God's grace. The divine

WEST POINTER TO IMPRISONED PREACHER... WHY?

payment is made in full, and no human efforts are necessary. It's that simple.

Ken had to man up. He had to brace himself up as a man. He really had to gird himself up during the three months of inhumane treatments. He truly had missed his prescription bifocals. Taking them away for several months as a suicidal preventive measure clearly showed that the authorities had determined that Ken was mentally unstable where he might use his glasses to hurt himself. This was indeed outrageous.

However, when Ken braced himself up as a man and completely surrendered to his Creator, he had truly experienced the divine grace. He never gave up his faith in his Creator, but he often questioned His doings. Why would such loving God allow such horrible deaths to occur? Did He really allow the tragedy? Ken finally came to the realization that no matter what happened, God was, is, and will always be. He heard his Creator loud and clear that God was still in charge of all affairs. Even in the storms, Ken learned to praise his Creator.

Could Jesus be just partially God? Could Jesus be lying? Could his first disciples, the apostles, and countless martyrs sacrifice their lives for the lie of the millennium? After two thousand years, there are two billion followers of Jesus. Could they all be following the false gospel of the millennium? Ken is very much convinced that Jesus was God in flesh. Like Jesus promised in Matthew 28:19–20, His presence continues with His followers through His Spirit to spread the Gospel of Messiah Jesus, the Lamb of God. Ken's overwhelming and unwavering faith in Jesus is the ultimate answer to the "Why?" question.

Now the author wants to conclude this chapter by sharing the final concluding remarks by Dr. Anita Boss.

Conclusions

- There is ample evidence to indicate that Mr. Yi was suffering from a severe mental disorder at the time of the alleged offenses.
- His mood disorder had been present and increasing in severity for at least six months prior to the alleged offenses and, possibly, for an entire year.
- Mr. Yi's mental disorder was characterized by severely depressed mood, severe insomnia, agitation, anxiety, ruminations, obsessive thinking, and psychotic features, primarily irrational thinking that reached delusional proportions and obsessions that were inconsistent with reality, with occasional mood-congruent hallucinations.
- Mr. Yi's personality and cultural issues influenced the expression of his mental disorder, though they were not caused of it.
- Mr. Yi's experienced intense, intractable shame, and disgrace due to a number of events in the three years prior to the alleged offenses. This contributed to the severity of his depression and the development of irrational thoughts that became fixed and further fueled the depression.
- From Mr. Yi's perspective, under the pressure of his severe mental disorder, his very existence had become such a burden to his family that he believed he had to die.
- There is ample evidence that Mr. Yi never fully acculturated to the United States, and thus, he believed his shame and depression brought shame and depression to his family.

- In the process of his mental disorder, he developed a fixed belief that, as his death would bring additional shame and hardship to his family, his only option was to kill them as well. He was unable to identify any alternative strategies to address his problems at the time of the alleged offenses.
- Mr. Yi's mental disorder was of a severity that his belief in any future resolution of his problems had collapsed, which was clearly an irrational belief.
- There are no indications that Mr. Yi had a history of violent expressions of anger nor is there evidence that he harbored anger of unusual proportions toward his wife or daughter.
- No alternative motivations of Mr. Yi to kill his family have emerged during this evaluation. Collateral information and the current evaluation indicate that his work and his family were the only things he cared about. As he believed he had failed at both his career and as a father and husband, he developed the irrational solution that they would all be in a better place if they were dead.

It is my professional opinion that, at the time of the alleged offenses, Mr. Yi was suffering from a severe mental disease that substantially impaired his ability to appreciate the nature, quality, or wrongfulness of his actions.

His condition impaired his access to rational thought to such an extreme degree that killing his wife and child made sense to him at the time. He fully intended to kill himself after they were dead, but he failed in two subsequent attempts [three more during ten-plus hours of distressful ordeal just prior to ingesting thirteen to fifteen Ambien pills].

Due to his mental disorder, he was unable to integrate his feelings, formulate plans to cope with them, foresee any improvements in the future, and identify strategies other than the one he chose at the time. As his emotions have settled and his thinking has cleared, he has been unable to explain his behaviors in rational terms, as it was the product of irrational thoughts directly linked to his mental disorder.

Dr. Anita L. Boss is Doctor of Psychology, Board Certified in Forensic Psychology, Licensed Clinical Psychologist, American Board of Professional Psychologists. Dr. Boss's final evaluation consists of twenty-five pages single space. In the beginning, the entire evaluation was considered to be included in this chapter; however, such measure would be counterproductive in meeting the I^3 purpose of this book. Ken fully agrees with Dr. Boss's conclusions, and our prayer is for the reader to make a sound judgment based on the tragic circumstances.

In summary, Ken has a message for the world. His message is captured in his speech delivered at the Buckingham Correctional Commencement. The short speech is printed in the last pages in this book.

The life may often seem unfair, unreal, or ungodly, but Ken preaches that the Creator or the Potter is minding His own businesses and that the creation or the humanity should also mind his or her own businesses. The purpose of the Creator for the humanity is to love the Creator God and also love the fellow humanity. When this purpose is realized and believed wholeheartedly, the world can enjoy a harmonious relationship with the Above and the Below as intended by the Creator God. May you enjoy such wonderful relationship!

Epilogue

Here the author wants to share Ken's most recent two memorandums written. His transformed life should become apparent as you read them. The reader should pay particular attention to Ken's message delivered at the prison's 2016 commencement ceremony. The message was delivered to inspire the audience, and it will close this book hoping to inspire the reader also.

May God transform your story regardless how trying it might be. May your story also touch the hurting lives of so many in the world. May you experience healing by serving fellow human beings. As Ken whole heartily preaches, the true healing comes by serving others.

PENUEL KODESH

December 20, 2016

Cypress Bible Institute
Dr. D. R. Vestal
P.O. Box 1536
Van, Texas 75790

Re: Doctorate of Theology (Th.D) Public Speaking Course

Dear Dr. Vestal,

 To earn some credit for the "Public Speaking" course in the Th.D program, the following public speaking is documented:

Date: December 9, 2016

Audience: Attended by 52 Veterans Support Group (VSG) members, two prison staff, and a community sponsor, Vietnam veteran and active minister.

Topic of the message: "Coming Out of Closets."

Duration: approximately 15 minutes.

Purpose: clearly stated "to excite and inspire the group."

Delivery: the stated purpose was met where the group gave undivided attention, participated in the discussion, and voluntarily gave a rousing applause at the end.

WEST POINTER TO IMPRISONED PREACHER... WHY?

Summary of the message: a humane and inspirational message of coming out of closets to heed to the divine call to serve others. First closet to keep secret was a major suicidal depression that I no longer have. Second closet was the military rank (a retired US Army Lt. Colonel), education (a West Point graduate), and a survivor of the 9/11 attack at Pentagon which I did not want exposed in prison. Last closet was the calling by the Lord Jesus Christ as His minister to serve people about which I did not want fellow prisoners to know. By coming out of these closets, I was set free to serve the people, especially fellow veterans living in the same pod and the rest.

I will have more public speaking next year, and I will so inform you to consider giving me some credit toward the "Public Speaking" course. Thank you!

Sincerely in Christ,
Kenston K. Yi
Candidate, Th.D and M.Div
JoeAnna Ministries
Cc: Ms. Anna Park

/signed/
Mr. J. R. Clark
President, VSG
/signed/
Mr. W. Buie
Secretary, VSG
/signed/
Ms. K. Craft, Librarian
Supervisor of the Signatories

February 2, 2017

*Cypress Bible Institute
Dr. D. R. Vestal
P.O. Box 1536
Van, Texas 75790*

Re: Doctorate of Theology (Th.D) Public Speaking Course

Dear Dr. Vestal,

To follow-up on your email to recognize some credit for the "Public Speaking" course of the ThD program, I would like to document the following public speaking moment:

Date: November 18, 2016

Audience: Attended by over 150 fellow prisoners, family members, friends, the prison leadership and staff including special honored guests (Enclosure 1)

Topic of the message: "Accolade and Inspiration."

Duration: approximately 10+ minutes.

Purpose: clearly stated "to encourage and inspire the audience."

Delivery: the stated purpose was met where the group gave undivided attention, voluntarily gave a rousing applause at the end of the message, and pro-

vided encouraging positive feedback from a number of attendees.

Content of the message: Although the prepared message (Enclosure 2) was only five minutes long, the impromptu portion of the speech before the main message was inspiring to me and the audience as I personally sensed in my spirit and as I so declared in the introduction.
As I should have more public speaking opportunities in the future, I will so inform you to consider giving me additional credit toward the "Public Speaking" course. Thank you!

Sincerely in Christ,
Kenston K. Yi, Th.M & BB
Candidate, Th.D & M.Div
JoeAnna Ministries
Cc: Ms. Anna Park

Enclosures:
1 - Graduation Program (not included in the book)
2 - Message

/signed/
Ms. K. Craft, the Librarian
/signed/
Dr. W. Lyle-Jones, the Principal

A Brief Remark for the Graduation Ceremony (Nov. 18, 2016)

By Kenston K. Yi, Th.M Cum Laude

Hello, honored guests, fellow graduates, family members, and friends,

I am so delighted and humbled to stand before you. I am here to give all of us a pat on our backs and inspire ourselves to make differences in our own lives and the neighborhoods we live in.

First, let us all be proud of our academic achievements. I am calling out all of us gathered here together to be proud of this wonderful graduation ceremony. We did it together! We, the graduates, could not have accomplished our academic goals without the support from the education system, praying family members, friends, and the resources provided by hard working Virginian taxpayers. So let us all be proud of ourselves for a job well done. In this noble regard, I sincerely thank you, all of you!

Second, we all have much more work to do because our Creator has given us breath to go on. So we should not sit idling waiting for something just to happen. One poet wrote a song about our calling, "God, with so much trouble in this world, why aren't you doing something? Then, God said, I did…I have created you!" How about Jesus's saying, "In this world, you will have troubles. Be of good cheer! I have overcome the world." Whether we believe in Jesus or not, the words of the poet and Jesus should inspire our hearts. Yes, we are more than capable to do something positive because more than able is on our side.

Shall we start by being of good cheer in our own lives and the troublesome world we live in? Because we are more than capable with more than able on our side, we can hopefully face tomorrow. Our families, our friends, the whole world, and, of course, our cheer Giver, are counting on us! As we step out to make a difference cheerfully, may we all be blessed in the Name of the cheer Giver whom I personally believe to be Lord Jesus! Respecting your own faith and asking for your respect also, I humbly pray. The Lord bless and keep you! The gracious Lord gives you His peace and good cheer! Thank you!

A Synopsis of the Story

A heartrending story of one ordinary man's audacious journey as a naive fifteen-year-old immigrant boy from war-torn South Korea, a dishwasher and a busboy during high school, an enlisted infantry soldier during the Cold War, a daring cadet at the prestigious United States Military Academy at West Point, a thirty-year veteran of an illustrative military career, a survivor of the 9/11 terror attack and a sufferer of an aggravating mental illness brought on by the attack, a victim of the broken VA medical care system, an incarcerated prisoner from a fatal family tragedy stalked by the failed system (in the mind of the author), a called minister of the Christian gospel during imprisonment, and a visionary to fulfill a God-given global outreach serving the hurt, both visible and invisible, through the Joyful Mission Network.

The Purpose of the Book = I³

Inform serious mental diseases, Illuminate the scriptures, and Inspire the reader to overcome the diseases by serving others.

What's Hot Next?

Many "How did he do it?" questions have been asked during the writing, editing and publishing this book. How did a 15 year-old immigrant learn English so fast to not only enter West Point in seven years, but also graduate from such competitive institution in four years? How did Ken manage to earn two master's degrees and study to earn the doctorate of theology degree while incarcerated? Next book, "West Pointer to Imprisoned Preacher...How?" should answer these intriguing questions and more. Meantime, Ken asks for your prayers.

About the Author

The first name, Penuel, comes from the story of Jacob's wrestling with "a man (Gen. 32:22-32)" all night. Jacob called the ground where he struggled with the man, "Penuel," whose Hebrew meaning is "face of God." The last name, Kodesh, comes from the story of the "burning bush (Exodus 3:1-12)" in Mt. Sinai or Horeb. God called the ground "Kodesh" whose Hebrew meaning is "holy." Since Hebrew is read from right to left, Penuel Kodesh means "Holy Face of God."

Hopefully, the author's name becomes divinely apparent as the reader flips through the book in relation to his or her Creator as Kenny Rogers's beautiful poem, "Mary Did You Know," subliminally echoes. This song has been beautifully sung in the radio, internet and TV media.

"Did you know that your baby boy
Has walked where angels trod?
And when you kiss your little baby
You've kissed the face of God."

As you prayerfully read this book
You've gleamed the Holy Book.